THE RIGHT THING

The Right Thing

Conscience, Profit and Personal Responsibility in Today's Business

By Jeffrey L. Seglin

SPIRO PRESS, 2003

First published in 2003 by
Spiro Press
17–19 Rochester Row
London
SW1P 1LA
Telephone: +44 (0)870 400 1000

ISBN 1 904298 97 4

British Library Cataloguing-in-Publication Data.
A catalogue record for this book is available from the British Library.

Library of Congress Cataloging-in-Publication Data on File.

Spiro Press USA
3 Front Street, Suite 331
PO Box 338
Rollinsford NH 03869
USA

Typeset by: Wyvern 21 Ltd
Printed by: King Printing, Lowell, Massachusetts
Cover design by: Alicen Brown

To
Evan and Luke, who bring me joy
and
Nancy, who makes the world seem right

Acknowledgments

'The Right Thing' column began as an idea tossed at me in 1998 by Jim Schachter, then editor of the Money and Business section of the Sunday *New York Times*. He championed the column through its early days, a role that was taken over by Judith H. Dobrzynski, when she succeeded him as editor of the section. First Patrick Lyons and then Vivian Marino were the editors at the *New York Times* who worked directly with me on the column each month. Their ability to challenge me resulted in a column that was better than it would have been if left to myself. My monthly conversations with Dan Cooreman, copy chief for the Money and Business section, added polish and clarity. And Paul Bolognese was the conduit through which all correspondence passed from readers to the paper to me.

The readers of 'The Right Thing' have regularly peppered me with tough questions or observations that rivaled the original column in their insightfulness. Some that have gone to extra lengths to give me feedback include: Nancy Austin, Wally Clausen, David Gebler, Larry Grimes, Jim Lewis, Jill Andresky Fraser, Cornelia Lewine, John Waggoner and George Zahka. The keen editorial eyes of Leslie Brokaw and Loren Gary have been particularly helpful.

At Spiro Press, Carl Upsall and Susannah Lear have been wonderful champions of the project. Spencer Smith of Book Network International is responsible for introducing me to Spiro Press and them to me. He and his business partner Jean Kerr have been unwavering in their enthusiasm for the book.

Aly Colón, Jeanne Nissenbaum, Bob Steele and Keith Woods of the Poynter Institute for Media Studies were wonderfully supportive during my time as an ethics fellow there. And my fellow ethics fellows continue to inspire me to work hard at being better at what I do as a writer and a teacher.

Emerson College has been my professional home since 1999. The administrators (particularly Dorothy Aram, Robin Fast, Mary Harkins and Grafton Nunes who freed up some time and resources for me), staff (particularly Emilia Dubicki and Kerrie Kemperman), and professor colleagues there continue to surprise me with how much attention they pay to what I do. The graduate students in the professional ethics seminar I teach were among those who added most to my thinking about how to approach 'The Right Thing' topics over the years. The most supportive of all my colleagues at Emerson has been John Skoyles. He regularly reads the column and always emails me thoughtful responses regardless of the topic. Until he stepped down as chair of the department of writing, literature and publishing to return to full-time teaching at Emerson, John was the best boss I ever had.

My father, Lester, probably has the most complete collection of the column clipped from the newspaper itself. This was no easy feat given that he spent his Sundays hunting down one of the few copies of *The New York Times* that made its way to the small city in North Dakota where he lives. My son Ed and his wife, Lisa, were also close readers as were my daughter Bethany and her husband, David. I look to the four of them and the lives they've chosen to live as models of how people can and do make tough choices and live good lives. My grandsons, Evan and Luke, regularly remind me that there is more to life than teaching and writing.

The person who is most responsible for each of the columns on the following pages getting written at all is my wife, Nancy. Before each column was sent off to my editor, regardless of the time of day or night, she would read and critique them, offering insight gleaned from both her years as a professional editor and now as a psychologist. She continues to be the most intelligent and supportive partner a guy could ever hope for.

About the Author

Jeffrey L. Seglin's column, 'The Right Thing', on business and workplace ethics, has been appearing on the third Sunday of every month in *The New York Times* business section since 1998. In it, he has reported on topics ranging from the ongoing inequity in managerial salaries for women and the impact of cultural differences on bribery practices to the fallout from the Ford/Firestone dispute and the impact of stock options on the behavior of rank and file employees at Enron. In 2001, he also wrote a monthly business ethics column for *Fortune* magazine called 'The Righteous Stuff'. He is a regular contributor of commentaries to public radio's 'Marketplace' and has been a commentator on business ethics for C.N.N. He was also a 2001 Ethics Fellow at the Poynter Institute for Media Studies. He is the author of *The Good, the Bad, and Your Business: Choosing Right When Ethical Dilemmas Pull You Apart* (John Wiley & Sons, 2000), which was chosen as one of ten books by the European Foundation for Management Development for its Library on Global Responsibility. He is a contributing editor to *Folio:* magazine.

Seglin was a Resident Fellow at the Center for the Study of Values in Public Life at Harvard University during the 1998-1999 academic year where, in addition to researching a book, he conducted a year-long seminar among Harvard Business School and Harvard Divinity School students on ethics in business.

He is the Director of the Graduate Program in Writing and Publishing at Emerson College, where he is an assistant professor. Before starting at Emerson, he was an executive editor for *Inc.* magazine where he began writing his 'Black and White' features on business ethics in 1997.

Seglin holds a Master of Theological Studies Degree from The Divinity School at Harvard University and an undergraduate degree in English from Bethany College in West Virginia. He has two grown children, both of whom are teachers, and two grandsons. He lives in Boston with his wife, Nancy.

Contents

Introduction

In the summer of 1998, the U.S. economy was still in the throes of a boom. Unemployment was at an all-time low, the stock market at an all-time high, and fledgling dotcoms and nascent conglomerates were chucking all kinds of perks and incentives at top executives and rank and file employees alike. Stories in the business press encouraged us to be 'our own brand' and more than one magazine celebrated the unusual job titles that spoke to the importance that cultural quirkiness took alongside sound management practices. There was a palpable excitement in the air as well as a seemingly endless supply of capital to myriad businesses, some of which were based on models that never got around to mentioning how profits would be made or growth would be sustained. It wasn't uncommon for employees to queue up for Thursday afternoon massages or daily lunches prepared by a *sous-chef* brought in to feed the rank and file. All was right with the world, and, at least to the hundreds of thousands who found themselves caught up in the frenzy, it just seemed as if all was going to get better and better.

That summer was also the time that Jim Schachter, then editor of the Money and Business pages for the Sunday *New York Times*, was working on a prototype that would totally revamp these pages. It would be full of the requisite business and economic news features, but it would also include an array of columnists bringing different voices and perspectives to the mix. At the time, I was preparing to head off on a year-long fellowship at the Center for the

Study of Values in Public Life at Harvard University. The fellowship would give me a year to do some research and analysis of how people in business make ethical decisions. I would work with graduate students from the Harvard Business and Harvard Divinity Schools in an effort to raise the questions and search for the answers that seemed part of the day-to-day ethical challenges of running a business. Jim asked if I would be interested in writing a monthly business ethics column that would come to be called 'The Right Thing'. We worked together on the first column for his prototype in July 1998. The actual first column would appear on the third Sunday in September 1998.

In the four years that have passed since writing that first column, the business climate has certainly changed. The heady days of an off-the-charts stock market and dotcoms chewing through a seemingly endless supply of capital have given way to massive layoffs, a burst dotcom bubble, and one major high-profile corporate scandal after another. What hasn't changed is the scope of the column (although the scandals certainly provide ample grist for the mill).

What we set out to do in the column was to raise ethical questions that people in business were likely to face themselves. Some were of the mundane day-to-day variety of how to make decisions about running a business. Others tackled large industry-wide issues or trends. Rather than write a screed each month that would chastise wrongdoers, the columns tried to help readers recognize some of the tougher questions that were raised by their actions. While I'd have a take on the point in each column, by reporting the pieces and interviewing both the people involved directly in the issues and expert outside observers, the goal at least was never to be preachy or didactic. Instead, at their most successful, the columns would get readers to think about issues more completely, or at least to think about them in ways they hadn't entertained before.

While I certainly wasn't the only one writing or thinking about business ethics at the time – as you can tell from the wide variety of voices that find their way into the columns that make up this collection – there wasn't, at least at the start, a great deal of coverage or discussion in the media about the role of ethics in making business decisions. That, of course, all changed dramatically with the introduction of Enron, Tyco, Imclone, Worldcom and a slew of other examples of bad behavior that became part of the daily lexicon of journalists and anyone involved in the world of business. Now, it's hard to go a day without finding mention of a new or old business scandal prospect on the front page of *The Wall Street Journal* and other major publications.

The result has consumed us with the topic. Top auditing firms caught up in one scandal or another are forced to rethink how they do business, if they're still in business at all. Companies rethink the worth of their own values statements when those of some of the major wrongdoers were among the best examples you could find. Top business schools began a more rigorous process to screen applicants for integrity by making sure that who they say they are and what they say they've done are not fabrications. The marketplace has been transformed into a place where players seem desperate to find a way to put integrity into their businesses, and are suspicious of those who say they already have it. The long and short of it is that there are no quick fixes. No ethics boot camps or political arm waving is going to fix business and set those who have strayed on the right path.

Over the past four years, I've cited in the column more than one survey or study that suggests how damaging misbehavior can be to creating a loyal workforce or building a profitable business. But using surveys to show why business leaders should behave ethically and actually follow the tenets of their own values statements or codes of ethics isn't likely to magically transform business. Top managers aren't likely to read survey results and then smack themselves on the forehead and say, 'Gosh, *that's* where I went wrong. I've got to get some ethics.'

Decision making has always been a process. We assess the situation, weigh up the options, anticipate the effect of our choices on all involved, and then take action. Done well, decision making always has an ethical component. We're often faced with making choices that might have a positive impact on one constituency but a not-so-positive impact on another. That's part of what makes managing a business successfully such hard work. Wrestling with the issues raised in the columns that follow can help readers exercise their decision-making muscle.

Something not to be overlooked in the effort to run a business well is how important it is to find the right people. While this seems obvious, too often too little time is taken when hiring people to get a sense of how they think about difficult issues or how their behavior might fit in with the company. No amount of ethical training or brilliant code writing can overcome a manager or employee who simply acts on his own self-interest, even when he knows his actions cross over ethical and legal lines. A challenge for managers is to spend time up front trying to ensure that they find people whose past behavior and current views mesh with the kind of behavior they want in their workplace.

A corresponding challenge arises when too little time is spent on hiring good employees. That, of course, is the ability to fire employees who don't measure up. Most managers, of course, would sooner do anything than fire an employee for any reason. When they don't, particularly when the employee has engaged in questionable behavior, the message goes out to the rest of the workforce that such behavior is tolerated. As a result, you often end up with a morale problem as well as the risk that the wayward employee will strike again. When managers fail, they shirk their own ethical responsibilities to the company, its employees and the people with whom they do business. Being a good manager is indeed always a challenge. Thinking through the ethical implications of their actions or inactions increases the challenge.

Given the current climate of high-profile ethical misconduct, it might seem as though those challenges to management are greater than ever. As you'll see from the columns that follow, that isn't so. Company builders face ethical challenges in both good economic times and bad. The trick is to act ethically, even when no one is watching.

The columns collected in *The Right Thing: Conscience, Profit and Personal Responsibility in Today's Business* explore some of the challenges facing business today. They appear as they did when they first ran. The job titles, company sizes and other facts about the people and organizations cited throughout the text appear as they did when the columns first ran (which accounts for some people having a different job title in various parts of the book). I have included some updating footnotes when it seemed relevant to the story. The issues raised are as relevant today as they were four years ago or a month ago.

The book is organized into six different parts: I. Ethics Policies and Life in the Corporation; II. Hiring; III. Bosses; IV. Privacy; V. Lying, Cheating and Stealing, and VI. Leading by Example. Each part is introduced by a brief comment on the topic. The date on which each column originally appeared is included at the start of each entry (chapter). Also included at the end of the book are a bibliography of sources and a list of resources mentioned throughout the collection.

Some of the columns have been used as points of discussion in business school classes as well as in corporations. While the columns raise issues and present options for action, they are by no means the final word on the topic. The discussion of ethics in business is one that at its best should be ongoing and always challenging assumptions. As such, I welcome your comments and reactions to the pieces that follow. You can reach me by email at jseglin@post.harvard.edu.

Jeffrey L. Seglin, Boston, Massachusetts, October 2002

PART 1

ETHICS POLICIES AND
LIFE IN THE CORPORATION

The ten chapters (columns) that make up the first part of *The Right Thing: Conscience, Profit and Personal Responsibility in Today's Business* each look at how policies or practices in companies raise dilemmas or challenges for managers and employees.

Some of the chapters look explicitly at a company's written code of ethics, albeit from a variety of different angles. In Chapter 2, 'The Values Statement vs. Corporate Reality', I touch on how the expectations and demands that a company places on its employees can send out a completely different message from its written values statement. The end result can wreak havoc on employee morale and behavior. Chapter 3, 'A Company Credo, as Applied or Not', looks at what happens to a company when its values statement shows signs of being challenged by behavior within the company, and how the company responds. Chapter 4, 'The Ethics Policy: Mind-Set Over Matter', features an analysis of some surveys of employee behavior in response to their perceptions when management doesn't behave in a way that coincides with the company's values statement. Chapter 10, 'An Ethics Code Can't Replace a Backbone', is a story about an organization's attempts to put a code of ethics in place after the behavior of one of its top managers is found wanting. The challenge for the company is to put a code in place while making sure that the way management reacted to the misbehavior jibes with what it says is appropriate behavior among all employees.

Two of the chapters look explicitly at the impact the issuance of stock options might have had on employee behavior. In Chapter 1, 'Do Stock Options Buy Silence?', the role that the issuance of stock options throughout an organization might have had in keeping employees from coming forward when they witnessed wrongdoing is featured. Chapter 9, 'Giving Advice Through Rose-Colored Stock Options', looks specifically at the potential conflicts of interest that might arise when outside consultants – specifically attorneys – are compensated for their advice with stock options.

The remaining chapters consider how some company policies or practices raise challenges in management's relationship to employees. Chapter 5, 'In Ethics, It's The Thought That Counts', looks at whether companies set policies about gift giving in their offices and what conflicts the presence or absence of such policies suggest. In Chapter 6, 'Between Consenting Co-Workers', the issue of policies regulating relationships in the workplace is raised, and whether such policies are appropriate. Chapter 7, 'Regulating Religious Life in the Office', stems from an incident involving an employee whose foul language offended a colleague and how a manager's decision to invoke the Ten Commandments may not have been the best response. And, finally, in Chapter 8, 'Playing It the Company Way, After Hours', the fairness of a company program that asked employees to perform work on their own time is explored.

1

Do Stock Options Buy Silence?

The New York Times, FEBRUARY 17, 2002

A question lingers as the Enron debacle unfolds: why did so few of the company's 20,000 or so employees come forward to report that something was amiss? Granted, not everyone would have had access to information about lapses in accounting judgment or would know if decisions were made to mislead rank-and-file employees about the financial health of the company. But it's a safe bet that hundreds, perhaps thousands, of employees saw some red flags or had an inkling that something was awry. What went wrong?

One explanation is that whistle-blowers in any corporate environment run the risk of being ostracized and forced out of the company, essentially committing career suicide. It takes a person of extraordinary conviction to come forward when there are few if any incentives to do so.

It's also true that when a company's stock is performing monstrously well, few people want to rock the boat, even if they know that shortcuts may have been taken.

That leads us to the subject of stock options. There is a growing trend among companies to issue such options to rank-and-file employees, not just those in the executive suite. Estimates put the total number of American employees holding them at roughly 10 million. Stock options are heralded as a way to motivate employees to work harder. Options are also used by start-up companies that are short on cash but want to lure prospective workers with the promise of future riches should the company's stock take off.

3

It's time, though, for companies to re-evaluate this practice.

At Enron, around 60% of the employees held stock options, according to Karen Denne, a company spokeswoman. But when so many people stand to lose if the stock price drops below a certain price, do they start excusing behavior that could diminish the stock if word got out?

'When a company's doing well, everybody says hands off,' said Nell Minow, editor and co-founder of the Corporate Library (www.thecorporatelibrary. com), a research firm in Washington, D.C., that monitors corporate boards.

Options, of course, are worthless unless a company's stock rises and stays above the strike price at which an employee was issued the options. So when a company's stock price is climbing, keeping tally of that stock price can become a consuming passion. Televisions in the elevators at Enron carried financial news stations that told employees how well the company's stock was doing, letting them compute just how wealthy they would be if they could exercise their options before they reached the next floor. (Forget the fact that option grants like those at Enron typically vest over several years. On paper, Enron elevator riders were growing richer as the stock price rose.)

The role of stock options in improving employee performance can also be questioned.

'You have to wonder whether having a stake in the stock market will really make the receptionist answer the phones more quickly, or with a more pleasant voice, or have the janitor sweep the room differently,' said Kevin J. Murphy, a finance professor at the University of Southern California in Los Angeles, California.

Of course, companies may decide to offer stock options for reasons that have nothing to do with employee motivation. A company may find options more attractive than other incentive plans because it does not have to show the options as a cost on its financial statements. And broad-based plans do not need the same approval from shareholders as plans issued solely to the top five executives, thus allowing extravagant options packages for those top executives.

If holding stock options can cause an employee to turn a blind eye to corporate problems, and if companies are being driven to offer them over other incentives because of favorable reporting treatment, it's time to take stock.

Companies must decide whether options are the best vehicles for motivating employees, when other measures actually pay for personal performance and do not reward silence.

'Options are very motivational,' Ms. Minow said. 'We just have to be a little more thoughtful about what it is we're asking them to motivate.'

True enough. If companies don't start becoming more scrupulous about their true intentions, then large institutional investors that control billions of dollars of shares in them will more than likely start moving their money elsewhere – and rightly so.

2

The Values Statement vs. Corporate Reality

The New York Times, SEPTEMBER 17, 2000

At the heart of the strike settled in 2000 between Verizon Communications and its telecommunications workers were the high stress levels experienced by service representatives. One possible culprit – and something not explicitly addressed by the settlement – was the fact that a company-wide values statement clashed with reality in the area of customer service.

The conundrum is common in business: how can a company ensure that a stated set of values, put into place to help drive it forward, does not conflict with that goal or with how employees are treated?

The core values in Verizon's statement, published in the company's newsletter, are integrity, respect, imagination, passion and service. One stark example of the disconnection at Verizon was the company's request that customer service representatives end each call with the scripted question: 'Did I provide you with outstanding service today?' Having just calmed an irate customer, a representative offering such a response – clearly tied to Verizon's core value of service – could set him off again. This request was cited by strikers as one cause of stress.

The problem with scripts is that they 'don't sound natural, and you wouldn't believe that I was even concerned about you,' said Melissa Morin, the president of local 1400 of the Communications Workers of America, based in Portsmouth, New Hampshire, and a customer service representative for Verizon and its predecessors since 1977.

More troubling, scripts, even if intended to promote better and more measurable service and sales, may fly in the face of Verizon's other stated values. What kind of imagination does a company value, for example, if it is asking service representatives to stick closely to a script? What kind of respect does it show for their abilities?

In the notes accompanying its values statement, Verizon said it had relied on the framework set out in the best-selling book, *Built to Last* (HarperCollins, 1994), which said that visionary companies have core values and a core purpose. But James C. Collins, its co-author with Jerry I. Porras, said that those values were not enough in themselves. The key 'is to preserve the core values and purpose, and stimulate change, improvement, innovation and renewal – at the same time, all the time.'

'Part of stimulating progress is giving people a lot of freedom to adapt to specific situations in the best, most progressive way,' he added. 'It sounds like the scripts were a very well-intentioned step, but a step that took away the freedom that's needed to truly live the values.'

James A. Smith, a Verizon spokesman, said that customer service representatives 'don't have to do anything by script,' and that the scripts were just a 'management tool of measurement.' 'Service representatives are taught to analyze the caller,' he added, 'and then lay against him a script that works to promote a specific product.' As Mr. Smith pointed out, their compensation is tied not only to whatever product is sold but also to how well customers, in later surveys, rate the service provided.

So the service representatives may be getting a mixed message about what the company really values. 'When there's such a strong incentive to meet a production number, in some sense you can be tacitly encouraging shortcuts,' said David Gebler, president of Working Values, an ethics training firm based in Boston, Massachusetts.

At Verizon, the conflict of such demands with stated values is not lost on employees – and has wide implications. 'Employees understand the values statement,' Ms. Morin commented. 'But I don't know that they believe the company is following its own words. They went into this micromanaging period where they started timing everything, picking every single word apart. People sort of just look at the values statement and go, "yeah, right. It's just a piece of paper".'

Values statements that do not reflect reality can do more harm than good, by fostering cynicism and anger. Rather than creating a statement just because great businesses do so, a company's managers may better spend their time finding what values exist within the company, and determining whether those values foster the type of company they want. If the answer is no, the managers should figure out how to respond.

'I'm not a big fan of the "right statement" model of the world,' James Collins said. 'I'm more a fan of the "get clear, skip the statement" part.'

3

A Company Credo, as Applied

or Not

The New York Times, JULY 15, 2001

Ralph S. Larsen[1], chief executive of Johnson & Johnson, clearly remembers his whereabouts on Tuesday, March 31, 1998. 'I was at a speaking engagement in Phoenix,' he remarked. 'I got a phone call that said: "Ralph, you're not going to believe this, but we just had a raid at our LifeScan headquarters by 30 or 40 armed federal agents. They've cordoned off the building and are serving a search warrant".' Larsen thought that the call might be an early April Fool's joke.

'It's no joke,' the caller assured him.

The raid came after management of LifeScan, a unit of Johnson & Johnson based in Milpitas, California, failed to notify the Food and Drug Administration

---

[1] Mr. Larsen retired as C.E.O. of Johnson & Johnson in April 2002.

of a glitch in software for the SureStep diabetes diagnostic device LifeScan makes. The defect caused some units to show an error message rather than a 'HI' warning reading if a person's blood glucose level was very high.

The United States attorney's office in San Francisco stepped in after a whistle-blower from LifeScan called the Justice Department. On December 15, 2000, Johnson & Johnson pleaded guilty to three misdemeanor criminal charges and agreed to pay fines of $60 million for selling defective devices and submitting false information about the problems to the Food and Drug Administration.

Johnson & Johnson is widely heralded for the values it displayed in 1982, when it decided to pull Tylenol off store shelves, at a cost of $100 million, after seven deaths were linked to bottles that had been tampered with. Was the LifeScan incident a sign that the company had lost its way?

'Mistakes were made in the LifeScan situation,' Mr. Larsen said. 'There were errors in judgment. We did too little, too late.'

Still, Mr. Larsen said his management team at LifeScan 'cared deeply about the company's credo', the one-page document written in the 1930s that sets out the company's values. It begins, 'We believe our first responsibility' is to customers, followed by employees, the community and, finally, stockholders. All 100,000 employees are expected to know the credo. It is at the heart of most management training at the company.

'Tylenol, in effect, made the credo,' said Michael Josephson, president of the Josephson Institute of Ethics in Marina del Rey, California. The Tylenol case also raised the bar for what people expected of the company.

Mr. Larsen acknowledged that sentiment, saying: 'More is expected of us than other companies. That's totally fair.'

The public still views the company positively. For a second consecutive year [2002], a Harris Poll has ranked it first among companies that Americans hold in high regard.

'They had a complicated device,' Mr. Larsen said of LifeScan management, all of whom have since left the company voluntarily. 'They felt it was the best on the market. Their interpretation was that the problems weren't serious enough to have to report them. The sad thing is they were probably right, but they should have gone to the F.D.A. and told them they had a problem.'

While Ralph Larsen does not see their actions as a breach of the company's credo so much as a case of bad judgment, Michael Josephson had a different view. 'They knew the product was defective,' he said. 'According to its credo, Johnson & Johnson shouldn't be knowingly issuing the product, even if it wasn't dangerously defective. If these individual managers had been more vigilant as to what the spirit of the credo is, they would have behaved differently.'

Johnson & Johnson has hired Mr. Josephson to create a case study based on the LifeScan incident that can be taught to the company's top managers. One goal is to ensure that dissenting voices are more easily heard. Ideally, the company will also build in procedures that encourage employees to call the C.E.O. directly if they suspect that a defective product is about to be brought to market.

'Is there some indication,' Mr. Josephson asked, 'that either the company has lost some of its commitment or that the viability of the credo has in some way been diminished by the current situation? The answer to the first is absolutely not. And the answer to the second is somewhat. But I've never seen anybody try harder to get it back.'

Precisely because the Tylenol response stands in such contrast, the LifeScan incident raises doubts among Johnson & Johnson's customers and its employees who expect more of the company – as they should. It also raises expectations that the company will respond swiftly and strongly to ensure that such an event does not happen again. The test lies ahead.

4

The Ethics Policy:
Mind-Set Over Matter

The New York Times, JULY 16, 2000

To read the news release announcing the results of the first KPMG Organizational Integrity Survey [Summer 2002], you would think that the American workplace had plunged into a deep ethical malaise.

'Employees are observing widespread illegal and unethical conduct in the workplace despite the presence of ethics programs,' the release began. Five out of six respondents said their companies had such programs; three out of four said they had observed unethical or illegal conduct on the job in the past year. The clear implication is that the programs are failing, right?

Hold on. One could just as easily conclude the opposite – that all those ethics programs have taught employees to recognize unethical behavior when they see it.

'I hadn't quite looked at it that way,' remarked Richard Girgenti, KPMG's national director of investigative and integrity management services. 'But yes, I would say that they may be more apt to know that what they're seeing is unethical as a result.'

Either inference would be a stretch, really, because no data is offered about the relationship between ethics programs and unethical behavior in the workplace over time. All we know for certain from the KPMG survey and one released in June [2002] by the Ethics Resource Center, a non-profit educational

11

and consulting organization in Washington, D.C., is that ethics programs, effective or otherwise, are nearly everywhere.

Nothing so clear can be said about the prevalence of misconduct. In the study by the resource center, only 31% of employees said they had observed misconduct over the past year. Whatever the reason for the discrepancy – eg varied definitions, survey methods and sample characteristics could all be involved – the gap is too large for me to take either figure as definitive.

A cynic would say that such surveys, whatever the results, are just grist for a full-employment call for ethics-program consultants: 'Your ethics policies aren't working? You need us. Working too well? You need us. Nobody in your industry has a program? You need us. Everyone else has a program? You need us.'

Perhaps. But with some extrapolating and postulating, it is still possible to glean an insight or two about the relationship between ethics and a company's bottom line.

In the KPMG survey, for example, 80% of employees who felt that management would uphold company ethical standards also believed that current customers would recommend the company to others. The figure falls by half among employees who thought management was not above giving the green light to a bit of impropriety. Now look at the figures for recruiting by word of mouth: 81% of employees who see their management as arrow-straight would recommend their company to potential recruits; only 21% with more, er, ethically flexible bosses would do so.

'Quite frankly, there's a link between how your employees perceive the ethical climate in which they're working and a company's key performance measures for profitability,' noted Laura Hartman, an adviser for the resource center survey and a business ethics professor at DePaul University, Chicago.

More broadly, both surveys indicate that a written ethics policy, in itself, is not enough to change behavior. Without a commitment from management and a way for people to report ethical lapses without fear of retribution, such policies may do more harm than good.

'A written policy without anything else is worse than not having a policy,' Hartman said. 'It really says, "Here's certain values, but we're going to allow you to break those values or infringe upon those values." It's like parents who have very strict rules, but they enforce them based on whether they had a good day or not,' she continued. 'For me, that's horrible. Not only does the kid never know if he's going to be disciplined or not, but he also doesn't learn what the real parameters are. In a company, that's very dangerous.'

If you really want to know whether company ethics policies are working, survey statistics may just be a distraction. 'Ultimately, a successful program is not identified by whether misconduct is up or down or whatever,' said Kenneth Johnson, a senior consultant at the Ethics Resource Center. 'It's more whether people look at it and say, "Well, this is just the way we do things around here".'

5

In Ethics, It's the Thought That Counts

The New York Times, DECEMBER 19, 1999

With the holidays approaching, and after a grueling season setting up fund-raising campaigns, Kathleen E. Pavelka, chief executive of Telecomp in Rochester, New York, decided to do something special for her clients. She sent each of them a $50 American Express gift check with a note: 'For all the evenings spent at work, please enjoy an evening out on us.'

Within a few days, 2 of the 20-odd recipients returned the checks, saying that accepting them would violate their organizations' policies. 'It was embarrassing,' Ms. Pavelka said. 'I only realized in hindsight that several of the clients had a policy of accepting no more than $25 value gifts.'

But set aside the etiquette aspect for a moment. Gift policies are ostensibly about ethical behavior. Were the two returners conforming to a higher ethical standard?

Gifts given and received stir up a witches' brew of conflicting impulses and desires, in business no less than in personal relationships. Imperatives of manners, obligations, reciprocity and appropriateness converge on the giving of a business gift (here defined as gifts to people at other organizations – clients, suppliers, potential customers, etc – and not gifts to co-workers).

Most people like receiving presents, and giving them. That is a major reason they are given at all, though far from the only one. Setting limits on such a pleasant practice feels Grinch-like. So it helps to remember that it isn't the gift that presents the ethical issue; it's what is implicitly expected in return.

And something is always expected, whether it is being allowed to deliver a pitch ahead of a stingier – oops, make that 'less thoughtful' – rival, or being 'taken care of' when a vital component is in short supply or getting calls returned the same day.

On the receiving side, many companies want to send a message that their favor cannot be curried in this way. But they don't want to seem mean and puritanical. The usual result is a compromise: a dollar ceiling like the one Kathleen Pavelka's gifts fell foul of.

Executives who develop such policies, like Patrick J. Gnazzo, vice president for business practices at United Technologies in Hartford, Connecticut, acknowledge that there is no special significance about the amounts. (In his company's case, gifts worth $50 or more and meals worth $100 or more must be reported to a supervisor.) 'But you have to set a number,' he said, 'and it's what we considered to be a reasonable number.'

But do ceilings, however practical, get to the root of ethics issues? To borrow an old adage, once you are willing to accept a gift meant to alter commercial behavior, everything else may be just quibbling over price.

Patrick Gnazzo's company has a major exception to its policy: employees in procurement cannot accept gifts at all. But it is a ban rooted as much in cool business sense as in ethics. 'We would rather have the product be a product that is priced fair,' Mr. Gnazzo said of the company's relationships with suppliers. 'We don't need them to entertain us and buy us gifts, because that all goes into the cost of the product.'

Some people argue that businesses cannot afford to buck the culture. Mr. Gnazzo is not alone in observing that if a company chairman were to visit a country where 'gifts are being given and are customary, we're going to bring a gift and we're going to receive a gift.' Even if the gift is passed on to charity after the chairman flies home, the fact that gifts are expected in the course of business suggests that the practice is more than social nicety.

A telltale sign of ethical trouble is a policy that is harsher on receiving gifts than on giving them. In a 1996 survey, two out of five executives at large public companies said that their companies had such double standards.

Strict no-gifts policies – bans on giving or receiving – may look impractical, though Wal-Mart Stores seems to manage. It has banned gifts and gratuities of any value since its founding in 1962, to no obvious ill effect.

'Our relationships with our suppliers are very strong, very healthy and mutually respectful,' said John Bisio, a spokesman.

There may indeed be little real harm in accepting, say, a $40 bottle of wine from a supplier or sending a $60 ham to a client. Maybe you can remain impartial afterwards; who, after all, can be bought so cheaply? But why not stop pretending that there is a strict line between safe and unsafe business gifts, and acknowledge that they all come with strings attached? Then, at least, you are being honest about it – as long as you declare them to the Internal Revenue Service (I.R.S.).

6

Between Consenting Co-Workers

The New York Times, SEPTEMBER 20, 1998

Not a day had gone by in the fall of 1998 when I hadn't read in the paper, received an email or heard in conversation that any corporate chief executive who was caught having a consensual relationship with a young intern or staff member – behavior that mirrored President Bill Clinton's – would be given the heave-ho.

Hogwash.

'In the cases that I've been reading, that's just not so,' remarked Carol Sanger, a professor of law at Columbia Law School in New York City, who teaches courses on sex discrimination and family law.

Certainly, when sexual harassment does occur, more and more companies are rightly taking a strong stance against the perpetrator. But when it comes to 'inappropriate relationships' between consenting parties, the picture is far less clear.

Most companies have no written policy on workplace romance. In a January [1998] survey by the Society of Human Resource Management, 72% of human resource professionals said their company had no such policy, written or unwritten. And of those whose companies did have a policy, more than half said it discouraged but did not forbid office romances. The most likely outcome of such a romance, they said, was marriage.

The ethical issue facing chief executives, boards, company owners and managers should not be whether an executive who dates an employee half his age ought to keep his job; it should be, 'What effect does this behavior have on our company and, no less importantly, on the rest of our employees?'

Framed that way, the issue poses three main challenges:

- How can companies address workplace romances so that all parties are dealt with humanely?
- How can companies ensure that any condoned behavior does not jeopardize people's professional careers?
- How can companies prevent employees from using rank and power to trap others into relationships they do not want?

Most companies, though, do not see the problem as an ethical issue, but rather as a liability limitation exercise – avoiding the sexual harassment lawsuits that can spring from an office romance gone sour, or from other employees who feel discriminated against for failing to bed the boss.

'We live in such a litigious society, where people are so willing to make claims,' said Nancy E. Pritikin, a partner in the San Francisco, California, office of Littler Mendelson, an employment law firm. 'And the claims are so expensive to deal with – even when you win them – that companies are really struggling with ways to avoid the problem.'

Some companies that permit relationships between supervisors and subordinates now insist that the supervisor report the relationship to the human resources department. Then both parties are asked to sign a contract acknowledging their consent to the relationship. These 'love contracts' may seem a ridiculous way to treat adults but they show that companies have at least begun to grapple with a difficult issue.

Policies about sexual harassment are fairly clear-cut to draft: most people agree it's bad. But when it comes to the appropriateness of workplace romance, the issue gets murkier.

'I don't know whether our society is prepared to take the step of saying you cannot date anyone you work with,' Ms. Pritikin said. 'But disclosure is one step in the right direction for the manager, company and individual, so they can be sure that no one's being taken advantage of. Sure, we're talking about pretty private behavior here,' she continued. 'But when you're a manager or a supervisor, you can't expect that you can have a completely private relationship with a person at work who reports to you.'

Professor Sanger of Columbia Law School observed: 'No one knows quite what to do. But it's ridiculous to think that people at work aren't going to fall in love.'

True enough. Companies must decide what role they will have in letting them.

7

Regulating Religious Life
in the Office

The New York Times, MAY 16, 1999

'If you've studied history, religious wars are the longest, nastiest and bloodiest.'

That observation comes from Charles E. Corry, a 60-year-old Buddhist and former Marine who has sued the Analysts International Corporation (A.I.C.), saying he is a victim of religious discrimination.

Dr. Corry's case is part of a growing number of such complaints reaching the courts or the Equal Employment Opportunity Commission (E.E.O.C.) – nearly 1,800 in 1999, up 15% from the year before. But his is no garden-variety case, and it casts a telling light on the difficult ethical terrain surrounding religion in the workplace.

Dr. Corry, a database consultant, was not turned down for hiring or promotion because of his faith, which is what 'religious discrimination' conjures up for most people. And he wasn't involved in a dispute over proselytizing, which is the most common religion-related problem at work.

This more ambiguous case stems from events in the fall of 1995. As Dr. Corry tells it, when a particularly devout Christian co-worker complained about his use of language that included epithets laced with references to God, an A.I.C. manager told him to conduct himself in accordance with the Ten Commandments.

'I said: "I don't think I'm going to do that. I'm not a Christian. I've been a Buddhist since about 1958 or '59"' Dr. Corry said in an interview. Technically, Dr. Corry was a contract employee working for Quest Database Consulting on a project for US West in Denver, Colorado; A.I.C., based in Minneapolis, Minnesota, had been hired to supervise contract employees like him. So, after the incident, Dr. Corry wrote a letter of complaint to Quest. Before the week was out, he said, he was told by Quest that the A.I.C. manager had terminated his contract.

He then filed his religious discrimination claim with the E.E.O.C., arguing that he had been sacked for objecting to being told to follow the tenets of a religion not his own. Analysts International countered that Dr. Corry's language was offensive to his co-workers' religious beliefs. The Ten Commandments were brought up solely to illustrate why someone might take offense, said the company's lawyer, Charles E. Jones.

In that light, Dr. Corry's case isn't about discrimination so much as balancing competing rights and sensibilities that, increasingly, are clashing head-on in the workplace. Where does an ethical compass point when respecting one person's religious beliefs involves offending another's?

Dr. Corry thinks the compass should point out the door. Religion in the workplace 'is messy and ought to be kept completely out.'

But that's not in the cards, practically speaking. 'The workplace has taken the place of neighborhoods, families and churches,' said Gil Stricklin, president of Marketplace Ministries of Dallas, Texas, which provides corporate chaplains to 170 companies. 'That's where your support, friends and relationships come from.'

But defining appropriate religious behavior at work can be tricky. Companies are usually on safe ground accommodating workers' desires for, say, Bible study groups at lunchtime, if participation doesn't become a *de facto* condition for employment or advancement. But courts have found that seemingly well-meant gestures like mailing out Bible verses with paychecks can constitute harassment, because they impose religious messages with the force of the company's voice on all workers, including those who don't want to listen.

Dr. Corry sued when settlement talks, prompted by an E.E.O.C. ruling in his favor, fell apart. But the jury that heard the case did nothing to clarify matters. It found simply that A.I.C. wrongly interfered with Dr. Corry's contract with Quest and awarded him damages of $34,160.

Both sides claimed victory. The company's lawyer said the jury found no discrimination or retaliation. Mark Bove, Dr. Corry's lawyer, said the jury had really found that A.I.C. wasn't technically Dr. Corry's employer and so had no liability under bias laws. Both sides are appealing[1].

---

[1] On June 6, 2000, the United States Tenth Circuit Court of Appeals overturned the jury verdict citing insufficient evidence that A.I.C. intentionally inferred with Dr. Corry's contract.

Certainly, the manager could have spared everyone a lot of trouble by reprimanding Dr. Corry over his language and leaving the Ten Commandments out of it. That might have kept the dispute out of the courts. But it would have left unaddressed the problem of whose beliefs to accommodate. 'Just as you don't tie your problems in a neat little package and leave them outside the gate at the plant,' Mr. Stricklin said, 'you don't leave your faith out there either.'

8

Playing It the Company Way, After Hours

The New York Times, FEBRUARY 20, 2000

Management at the Bank of America thought it was on to a winner. In a program called 'Adopt an A.T.M.,' begun in June 1999, the bank asked employees to volunteer to look after one of its automated teller machines and to keep the machine's surroundings gleaming with pride – on their own time and without pay.

'We thought it was a great idea,' said Kieth Cockrell, executive vice president in Charlotte, North Carolina in February 2000, of the bank's credit, debit and smart-card division, which oversaw the program. More than 2,800 of the bank's 158,900 workers signed up to adopt one of the bank's 10,000 teller machines.

But when Marcy V. Saunders, the California state labor commissioner, read about the program, she hit the ceiling. She wrote to the bank, saying the program seemed to be in clear violation of 'basic precepts of wage and hour law' and demanding that the volunteers be paid or that the program be discontinued within ten days. The bank met with Ms. Saunders to see if it could satisfy her objections, but rather than comply with the requested changes, it suspended the program and instead set up a toll-free number for employees to report problems at A.T.M.s.

Even if asking employees to work for nothing were legal, though, the program would have raised important ethical questions about the nature of the company–employee relationship. Not least is the issue of reciprocity. Does an employer that counts on its workers to further its interests during their own time, *gratis*, have a right to discipline workers who handle personal business during office hours?

'Companies feel perfectly free to infringe upon employees' time, while not necessarily being extremely flexible when it comes to employees' demands for time,' remarked Daryl Koehn, director of the Center for Business Ethics at the University of St. Thomas in Houston, Texas.

On this front, Bank of America's policy is fairly vague. 'In our code of ethics,' said Ann L. DeFabio, a bank spokeswoman, 'basically it just says that the proper use of Bank of America assets is essential to the financial soundness and integrity of the bank.' But it is not likely that a large bank would see much equivalence between, say, employees' using company postage to pay personal bills and using their own paper towels to clean A.T.M. screens.

It is a common ethical disconnect. Most businesses think nothing of expecting extra miles from employees, and are shocked when it's drawn to their attention. They automatically think of the employee's commitment to the company as open-ended, but draw a sharp line around the company's commitment to the employee.

Some critics see cynical, deliberate exploitativeness in such attitudes. By and large, I don't doubt the employers' good intentions – just their logic. Still, plans like 'Adopt an A.T.M.' bespeak a patronizing arrogance, an assumption that company pride is reason enough for employees to give and give some more – never mind whether the company gives anything back.

'Quite often the leaders really are doing what they think is in the best interests of the company,' said Michelle L. Reina, co-author of *Trust and Betrayal in the Workplace* (Berrett-Koehler, 1999). 'They do at times tend to forget the individuals involved. When they get the type of response they're getting in this particular case, they are caught off guard. And at times they feel betrayed in response.'

On the surface, such indignation might seem justified. 'From an ethical perspective, Bank of America is doing nothing wrong' with the program itself, said Laura P. Hartman, a professor of business ethics at the University of Wisconsin. 'The ethical issues come up where there is undue influence of an inappropriate nature.'

That is a potentially fatal flaw inherent in any 'voluntary' program handed down from management, particularly one tied to company business: there is subtle coercion just in asking, because some employees won't feel free to say no, regardless of how big the word 'voluntary' is on the flier.

Employees who truly love the bank enough to volunteer freely for such a program are probably already picking up any litter they find near an A.T.M. – without having to be asked. Beyond that, all a formal adoption program could accomplish is inducing less-than-willing employees to join the unpaid tidiers. That's why it struck so many as unfair.

9

Giving Advice Through
Rose-Colored Stock Options

The New York Times, DECEMBER 17, 2000

As dotcom companies hurried onto the public markets during the internet stock run-up of the late 1990s, everyone wanted a piece of the action. Not only were the companies' founders sitting on a potential pot of gold in their equity, employees also got in on the possible upside by holding stock options. And the options booty was also extended to outsiders, like lawyers and consultants.

Dotcom stocks, of course, have taken a tumble since those heady days, and options are not as attractive – if they have any value at all. But that doesn't negate the need for many start-up companies to find alternative means of payment for services they receive. Cash, after all, is precious for day-to-day operations, so many dotcoms continue to use shares or stock options to pay outside vendors and consultants.

For an outsider who supplies a tangible product in exchange for equity, such deals pose few conflicts. But what if the outsider is in the business of providing objective advice – about when to go public, for example? Could such advice be tainted by the self-interest of reaping a big pay-off from the company's initial public offering?

The quandary is front and center when lawyers accept stock or stock options in a company instead of cash for their advice and services.

'It pits human nature to be professional versus human nature to look out for oneself,' said Jeffrey Haas, professor of securities law at the New York School of Law. 'Both are very strong primitive notions.'

But paying with stock can make economic sense for a new business. 'In the beginning of a company's life, equity becomes the only currency you have to buy top-flight services,' said Fred Marcusa, a senior partner at Kaye, Scholer, Fierman, Hays & Handler in Manhattan.

Mr. Marcusa still receives only cash for his services. But he says many people who give advice can be influenced by the simple fact that they are paid – whether in cash or in stock. He said he thought the conflict over lawyers taking stock in lieu of cash resulted from 'a certain amount of jealousy' among people at other firms who didn't get in on the action.

Others reject outright the idea of receiving stock. 'I just don't do it,' said Gerald E. Boltz, a partner in the Los Angeles, California, office of Bryan Cave. 'It has an impact on objectivity. The company is entitled to objective legal advice. I'm not sure it's good for the company or the attorney.'

While the American Bar Association (A.B.A.) has decided that there is nothing illegal or unethical about lawyers taking stock in lieu of cash, it has set only broad parameters: the transaction must be reasonable, the client must consent to the transaction in writing, and the client must have reasonable opportunity to seek a second legal opinion on the deal.

Recognizing that some companies may not have the wherewithal to pay a top lawyer in cash, the A.B.A. suggests that if stock is used, the amount should be equal to the cash value of the services, based on the stock price at the time of the transaction. But many people see a qualitative difference between taking cash and taking stock of comparable value, especially in a hot market. 'It's like swinging for the fence,' Professor Haas said of accepting stock. 'If, normally, you're getting $300 or $400 per hour for doing this type of work, if the stock turns out to be a home run, it could turn into $1,500 an hour, in essence.'

That something is ethical simply because it's socially acceptable is an arguable point. Ethical conflicts become clearest when the pay-off from going public is huge.

'It's not the form of compensation you want to keep your eye on, but the relative magnitude,' said William H. Simon, a professor of legal ethics at Stanford Law School. 'If a large fraction of a lawyer's portfolio is invested in a client, then people worry that his independence will be compromised and he'll be more likely to overlook improper practices or even encourage them in the hope of personal gain.'

When the stock market settles down, the conflict isn't as clear, and neither are the concerns of the lawyers who accepted the stock. Lawyers shouldn't be asking themselves whether to take stock instead of cash, but rather when to drop clients who don't pay in cash.

The real issue isn't whether there is a conflict in accepting stock compensation. Of course there is the potential for conflict. The challenge is how to deal with it.

10

An Ethics Code Can't Replace
a Backbone

The New York Times, APRIL 21, 2002

The parent company of *The Harvard Business Review* is writing a code of ethics. Walter Kiechel, editorial director of Harvard Business School Publishing, refers to it as 'tenets of community behavior.'

'If you violate this, you would be violating the norms of the community and the bonds of trust with colleagues,' he told me, describing the code's message.

It's no accident that these 'tenets' are in the works. A committee was formed to write them after it became known that Suzy Wetlaufer, the former editor-in-chief of *The Harvard Business Review*, had formed a personal relationship with Jack Welch, the former chief executive of General Electric, while interviewing him for a feature article in the magazine. (Her interview was replaced by one conducted by two senior editors.) Ms. Wetlaufer said on March 8, 2002, that she was stepping down as the editor-in-chief. But she was scheduled to return as an editor-at-large the week of April 21, though working from home for at least the following six months.[1]

Some people have suggested that writing the code is a little like closing the

---

[1] Two days after this column ran in *The New York Times* on April 21, 2002, Suzy Wetlaufer resigned entirely from *The Harvard Business Review* and Harvard Business School Publishing.

barn door after the horse has bolted. 'The biggest mistake people make,' said Michael Rion, a business ethics consultant in West Hartford, Connecticut, 'is trying to rewrite policies to solve last month's problem.'

Mr. Kiechel said that this was not the case, that there was no 'single arrow or thrust' behind the code.

Still, he and other top management must convince employees that the company is not using a code to brush aside past events and, more importantly, that it acts on what it says it values.

Linda Klebe Treviño, a professor of organizational behavior at Pennsylvania State University, said that outlining appropriate or inappropriate behavior in a code, with the intention of avoiding future problems, 'can be a healthy response.'

'But if you create a code, especially if it's in response to some problem, and it's inconsistent with the culture as employees perceive it, then it appears to be only window dressing and hypocritical,' she added.

After the disclosure of the problem at *The Review*, four editors there wrote to Walter Kiechel asking him to remove Ms. Wetlaufer from the publication. On March 8, after he decided not to do so, two senior editors resigned in protest.

'I found the decision to write a code of ethics laughable because of the wide gap between the ethics the organization professes and the ethics it practices,' said Harris Collingwood, one of the senior editors who resigned. 'It's a pretense of a commitment to open intellectual enquiry, equal standards of behavior for all people, a pretense of that without the practice of that.'

Not dismissing Wetlaufer for stepping across ethical lines raises the suspicion that senior management doesn't have the conviction to act on its stated values. That question applies whether the decision was made out of compassion or fear of a lawsuit backed by Jack Welch's deep pockets.

'When management disciplines somebody, they're sending a very powerful signal,' Professor Treviño said. 'Most people are going about their business trying to do the right thing. When they see somebody engage in highly inappropriate behavior, that everybody agrees is inappropriate, and management doesn't do much about it, it devalues the norm and, in a sense, their own status.'

No code can address all intransigent behavior. 'It's questionable whether the things that have brought this much attention on to *The Review* and the company in the last couple of months would have been effectively governed by any set of guidelines,' Mr. Kiechel said.

But what was firmly within the grasp of top company managers was the chance to send a loud and clear message that some behavior will not be tolerated from anyone.

'The point is not to second-guess the decision' to keep Ms. Wetlaufer on staff, Mr. Kiechel said of discussions he plans with employees after her return. 'It is to try to get a better shared understanding of just what our norms are.'

By keeping Suzy Wetlaufer on staff, however, Harvard Business School Publishing is sending the message that either she didn't violate the norms of the 'community' and the trust of her colleagues, or that she did and management didn't have the backbone to take action. If weak management is the case, then a new code of ethics, no matter what you call it, will ring hollow.

PART II

HIRING

Each of the six chapters (columns) in Part II touches on some aspect of the hiring process, including the prickly subject of firing.

Several of the chapters touch on the issue of loyalty. Chapter 11, 'An Offer You Can't Refuse. Well, Maybe', explores what responsibility employees have, if any, after they've accepted an offer from one employer only to find that a little while later a better offer comes their way. In Chapter 14, 'In Downsizing, Loyalty is a Two-Way Street', the effect that knee-jerk layoffs have on the trust between employer and employee is considered, particularly in the light of the flurry of layoffs that have occurred since the late 1990s. The

scenario painted in Chapter 15, 'As Layoffs Loom, Loyalties Are Divided', is of an employee asking for his boss's advice on a major personal expenditure when the boss knows, but has been asked not to tell, that the employee is on a list of those being laid off in a couple of weeks. The boss must make a decision about what to tell the employee and whether he has a greater loyalty to him or to the company as a whole.

Several of the chapters look at how fear of litigation too often becomes an excuse for not making the difficult ethical decisions managers must make in running a business. In Chapter 12, 'When Fear of Firing Deters Hiring', the legitimacy of the extreme caution that some managers express in hiring minority employees for fear of a lawsuit if the relationship doesn't work out is explored. Chapter 13, 'Too Much Ado About Giving References', also touches on whether a fear of litigation is legitimate. This time it concerns whether the practice of giving a complete, honest reference rather than name, rank and serial number (as many employment attorneys suggest) is grounded in a realistic concern about being sued over an honest, albeit negative, reference. Finally, in Chapter 16, 'In Dismissals, Silence Has Its Perils', maintaining silence over employees who leave the company, and its impact on those employees who remain, is featured.

11

An Offer You Can't Refuse.
Well, Maybe

The New York Times, JANUARY 21, 2001

A good employee is not only hard to find but also hard to keep. With the United States' unemployment rate holding steady in January 2001, at 4%[1] – the lowest in more than 30 years – it is no wonder that many employers are having a difficult time tracking down and retaining top talent. But as the offers and counter-offers fly, an ethical question arises: once you accept a job offer, is it ethical to go back on your word because someone else makes you a better deal?

Clearly, courting employees and making offers can be time-consuming and expensive. Anecdotal evidence from the Society for Human Resource Management, a trade group based in Alexandria, Virginia, suggests that employers need, on average, 50 days to fill a vacant position. The average cost of the process is $4,588, according to the Saratoga Institute, a human resources research and consulting firm in Santa Clara, California, although many top executive recruiting firms charge a fee of one-third of the candidate's total annual financial package. It is no wonder that an employer becomes upset when a dream candidate gets away.

It's perfectly reasonable for someone to want to shop around for a new job

---

[1] 5.7% at time of writing – August 2002.

from time to time, even if only to establish a sense of worth in the market-place. 'People do go on interviews for jobs they don't really plan on taking, but then wind up taking them,' said Amanda Bennett[2], 48, a former Atlanta bureau chief for *The Wall Street Journal*, who did precisely that before signing on in 1999 as managing editor of *The Oregonian* in Portland, Oregon. She likened such experiences in general to that of someone who goes on a blind date and ends up marrying the match, 'quite to the amazement of both'.

When people merely window-shop for positions, and ultimately stay put, executive recruiters miss out on hefty rewards. Still, they accept such practices. 'There's nothing wrong with poking your head outside and taking a look,' said Janet Tweed, chief executive of Gilbert Tweed Associates, an executive search firm in Manhattan. 'But once you acquiesce and accept the offer, ethically you should take that job.'

Everyone understands that during negotiations for a new job, neither side is totally forthcoming. It is a courting ritual, and either would be ill-advised to lay himself bare, warts and all, for the other to see. But, noted Laura Nash, a business ethics consultant and a senior research fellow at the Harvard Business School, 'they cross the line to unethical when they deliberately mis-state the situation to deceive the other side.'

It is not uncommon, however, for someone to accept a job offer, then receive a counter-offer from another company that is also courting him. But what should he do if his current boss walks into his office and smacks down a better offer?

Janet Tweed said that succumbing to such an enticement once you have made a commitment to go elsewhere is fraught with peril. The current employer, though successful in keeping you, may see your job hunt as a terrible breach of loyalty. 'In the 20 years I've been doing this, I've worked for any

[2] Amanda Bennett was named editor of the *Lexington Herald-Leader* of Lexington, Kentucky, in September 2001. She was elected to the Pulitzer Prize Board in 2002.

number of companies where, at the moment a counter-offer was made and accepted, the employer gave us the assignment to find someone to replace that person,' she said.

It could be a no-win situation. Once a candidate goes back on his word of acceptance, he may ruin his chances of ever working for the company that made the offer. The main reason isn't the time and expense of the courtship – or the lost productivity of having held a crucial position open for so long, only to have to reopen the search. After a candidate steps over that line and says 'yes', he has given his word, he has made a commitment, and he is ethically bound to take the position. Such breaches don't go down well and are not quickly forgotten.

Of course, anyone can have a change of heart from time to time. But the time for reflection and rejection should come *before* accepting the job. It's the fair way to treat the company making the offer and the right way for any prospective employee to act.

12

When Fear of Firing Deters Hiring

The New York Times, APRIL 18, 1999

Over the last few years, several people have spoken to me about their reluctance to hire people whose race, color, creed or national origin – or age, disability or sex – put them in protected classes under anti-discrimination law.

The reasoning goes this way: you have to be absolutely sure that someone in a protected class is the best possible candidate, because people in these categories can make your life miserable with litigation if you ever have to dismiss them.

'It's a dirty little secret' that people are thinking this way, said Tama Starr, president of Artkraft Strauss, a sign-making company in New York, and one of the few business people who has spoken out on the subject. Those who subscribe to these ideas 'have to choose between different protected classes and weigh the risk of hiring them,' she said, adding, 'This is a very obnoxious way to think.'

Managers are treading on swampy ethical terrain when they allow fear of possible problems to deter them from hiring apparently capable minority applicants – or to hesitate so long over a decision that a candidate loses interest or gives up in frustration.

The fear of discrimination suits is not wholly groundless. A 1997 survey conducted by the Society for Human Resource Management found that of the 616 personnel executives who responded, 53% said their organizations had been sued at least once by former employees in the last five years; nearly half of the 611 suits they reported involved claims of discrimination.

But Martha R. A. Fields, chief executive of Fields Associates, a management consulting firm in Cambridge, Massachusetts, said the risk of a suit is often an excuse that masks a deeper motive for not hiring people in protected classes. It is more likely, Ms. Fields stated, that managers really just feel safer hiring people like themselves.

Some people, she said, find it easy to think to themselves: 'If I know people who are like me, I know the good, the bad and the ugly about them. If I don't know them and I see images of them in the media, I'm, like, "Oh man, those black people, they might be welfare-dependent, or criminals, or crime victims. I don't know if I really want to bring that into my organization."'

Increasingly, such bias is economically irrational as well as unethical. 'The

36

demographics of this country are shifting in major ways,' Martha Fields noted, as minority groups, especially Hispanic people, account for a rapidly growing share of the population and its purchasing power. 'Consumers want to see people like themselves in organizations,' Ms. Fields said.

Another underlying problem is managers who are poor at managing. Some who voice these fears are simply afraid to fire anyone – not just someone in a protected class – and shy away from situations they perceive as requiring them to take a chance.

To avoid hiring problem employees from any group, managers just 'need to do a good job of checking resumes, identifying the time gaps and verifying simple facts,' said Mary C. Dollarhide, an employment lawyer with Paul, Hastings, Janofsky & Walker in Stamford, Connecticut. For $200 to $300, a manager can also get a criminal background check on a candidate and a docket search to see if he or she often files lawsuits. 'If you do your due diligence, you're going to stand a much better chance of not bringing in the gripers, complainers, bad actors and poor performers,' Ms. Dollarhide said.

But a thorough screening does not absolve managers of having to manage. 'If you get somebody in your midst whom you fail to discipline because you're afraid you're going to get slammed for having reprimanded someone in a protected class, well, guess what: the failure to do that is going to land you in exactly the same spot,' Ms. Dollarhide warned. 'If the employee is terminated, he can sue and you're left with no records to support your case.'

Much sound management translates into ethical behavior. Employees who are treated fairly, honestly and directly are both less likely to require dismissal and less likely to sue over it later.

That frees everyone to concentrate on the business they enjoy. 'I still believe that people are good and honest and they want to do a nice job,' said Ms. Starr of Artkraft. 'Having to fight through more stupidity just hampers everybody's humanity.'

13

Too Much Ado About Giving References

The New York Times, FEBRUARY 21, 1999

T ry to get a detailed reference on a prospective employee these days, and you're likely to hit a wall.

Most managers balk at giving anything but the most basic information about former employees. At larger companies, enquiries are usually referred to the human resources department, which will probably only verify dates of employment, according to a recent survey by the Society for Human Resource Management. Only 19% of the 854 respondents in the survey would give a reference-seeker a reason why an employee had left, and only 13% would say anything about work habits. Why won't people give substantive references any more? Because of a pervasive spoken or unspoken fear of being sued by former employees who take issue with what they've said – or failed to say.

But, according to C. Patrick Fleenor, a management professor at the Albers School of Business and Economics at Seattle University, 'the fear of being sued and losing is not well founded.' A study of Federal and state court records nationwide from 1965 to 1970 and from 1985 to 1990, found only 16 defamation cases arising from reference checks. And plaintiffs prevailed in only 4 of the 16, he said. (The study was conducted by Steven L. Willborn and Ramona Paetzold. A similar study – involving court decisions and settlements in

Washington, Idaho and Alaska during 1995 and 1996 – was made by Professor Fleenor with Peter Arnesen and Marlin Blizinsky.)

Scott Rechtschaffen, an employment lawyer at Littler Mendelson in San Francisco, California, said: 'Part of the reason you don't see so many of these cases, from the plaintiff's perspective, is that they're quite difficult to bring. There are real problems of proof.'

Still, Mr. Rechtschaffen's 'standard' advice, like that of most employment lawyers, is to 'give out minimal name-rank-and-serial-number-type information.' That goes for good workers as well as bad, he said, since sticking to neutral facts only for less-than-stellar former employees would get 'into the problem of the employee alleging, "Well, their failure to give me a reference is in and of itself a negative."'

Indeed, keeping quiet is sometimes as dangerous as speaking up. A Californian case involved a school that neglected to mention to a prospective employer that its former vice principal had been accused of molesting a teenaged student. After the former vice principal was accused of molesting a 13-year-old girl at his new school, the California Supreme Court ruled that the referring school could be held liable for that omission.[1]

But few of us are in the position of having to recommend child molesters (at least ones we know about). Despite widespread belief to the contrary, it is possible to give references safely and ethically – both positive and negative – as long as they are truthful. Of course, if you're malicious or retaliatory, or show bias towards a group of people protected by civil rights law, you're asking for trouble.

---

[1] 'California Court Finds School Districts Negligent in Providing Recommendations,' *Human Resources Report* (BNA, Inc.), February 3, 1997. The case citation is Randi W. v. Muroc Joint Unified School District, Calif SuperCt, No. S051441, 1/27/97).

The fact is that most people know they can still get the deal on prospective employees if they really want to.

To get or give a reference these days, 'you have to build a very Rashomon kind of convoluted Byzantine structure,' said Dr. Pierre Mornell, a psychiatrist and author of *45 Effective Ways for Hiring Smart* (Ten Speed Press, 1998).

'If a lawyer or H.R. person calls a manager or C.E.O. about somebody, they're not going to say anything,' Dr. Mornell said. 'But they will talk back-door with somebody at their own level whom they know.'

The former personnel director of a 5,000-employee company in northern California, who spoke on condition of anonymity, acknowledged as much: 'While our company's policy was name, rank and serial number, off-the-record references were given all the time.'

Gone are the days, however, when you could count on your reputation following you from job to job – for good or ill. For managers, hiring has necessarily become more of a game of dice, infused with suspicions about the veracity of any references received and fear about those given.

At least a dozen states are considering laws that would shield employers who give accurate information about former employees. But with lawyers and personnel departments already taking truthful discretion out of our hands, do we really want government stepping in, too? Wouldn't it make more sense to take some of the $5 billion spent on employment lawyers every year and put it towards freeing managers from fear of litigation by teaching them how to give fair, above-board references?

14

In Downsizing, Loyalty is a Two-Way Street

The New York Times, APRIL 15, 2001

I'm not particularly good at firing someone. I know few people who are. On the few occasions when I was part of a group of managers considering layoffs, the process was agonizing. I found it excruciating to sit down with a list of people with whom I worked every day and assess who might be expendable.

For me, at least, the underlying question was always whether what we were about to do was fair to the company, the employees and those of us who would stay. Deciding the right thing to do was never easy.

Now, as the economy has cooled and downsizing has heated up, the ethics of layoffs have once again come into sharp focus, not only for the managers making the cuts, but also for the remaining employees. The number of people that were laid off in the first three months of this year (2001) – 406,806 – was nearly triple the total for the same period of 2000, according to Challenger, Gray & Christmas, the outplacement firm in Chicago, Illinois. And the numbers show no sign of decreasing.

The payroll is often the first place companies look when trying to save a bundle. But growing evidence suggests that such a response can be myopic. A [2001] survey by Mercer Management Consulting of businesses that used cost-cutting as their primary strategy in the first half of the 1990s – a period that included a recession – showed that 71% failed to achieve profitable growth in the strong second half of the decade.

When employees recognize that layoffs may be more of a knee-jerk reaction than a smart business solution, 'there's a cost to that,' warned Bob Atkins, a vice president at Mercer Management.

'You're breaking trust with your people,' he said.

Consider, too, that the highest number of layoffs during the last decade came in 1998, amid the economic boom, according to Challenger, Gray. It is no wonder that employees question how much they owe to their companies.

'If the 1990s have taught employees anything, it's that no matter how much they give to these corporations, they will give them nothing back in return,' said Jill Andresky Fraser, author of *White-Collar Sweatshop* (Norton, 2001). 'Companies relied on aggressive cutbacks throughout the prosperous 1990s to give one more short-term boost to the bottom line. They looked at their employees as yet another disposable commodity that could be squeezed dry and then thrown out the door.'

Whatever the reasons for layoffs, what ethical responsibility do employers and employees have to each other? If a layoff is imminent, do those employees who know that they are safe owe any loyalty to the company? And do employers owe loyalty to employees who have knuckled down in tough times and helped the business survive?

'The notion of loyalty has been so battered that it is naïve – indeed, even somewhat disingenuous – to expect that employees will be loyal,' said Daryl Koehn, a professor of business ethics at the University of St. Thomas in Houston, Texas.

Even when they do stay, employees may feel betrayed by a company that demands more work of them and gives back little in return. 'When people don't feel a level of acknowledgment, that's when they really constrict and, in the most serious cases, very significant sabotage against the company begins to occur,' warned Michelle L. Reina, a management consultant and co-author of *Trust and Betrayal in the Workplace* (Berrett-Koehler, 1999).

When considering layoffs, a company certainly has an ethical duty to make sure its decision will be a responsible one for the business. It also has a duty to treat laid-off workers fairly, by providing outplacement services and reasonable severance pay, and to ensure that those who remain have the tools and support to do their jobs.

When an employee decides to stay with a company – even amid fear of layoffs – he has an ethical responsibility to continue doing the good work he has always done. If he truly believes he cannot do so, because of some breach wrought by the layoffs, he should resign. After all, his responsibilities to his company do not change even if his perceptions of his employer have.

'We don't have control over how an organization handles a layoff,' Ms. Reina said, 'but we do have control over how we choose, as individuals, to respond to it.'

15

As Layoffs Loom, Loyalties Are Divided

The New York Times, AUGUST 15, 1999

An employee asks your advice about whether or not to buy a house. You know that the company is planning layoffs, and that he is likely to lose his job.

Do you keep quiet? Stall? Drop a hint? Or come right out and warn him?

The quandary is likely to keep coming up: even with unemployment at a 30-year low, layoffs are occurring at a record pace, a result of mergers and takeovers.

It's a problem that could test even the best managers. On the one hand, the person sitting across the desk is about to make a move that could turn into a colossal nightmare. Certainly, your compassionate side is drawn to his plight. How could you not tell him? Besides, can a company, a faceless institution, be harmed by one tiny indiscretion?

But hold on. What about your responsibility to the company? Spilling the news may seem insignificant, but it carries risks. The employee might spread the word, making other workers nervous or even setting off an exodus. Furthermore, if the company is public or is merging with a public company, letting an employee know beforehand might fall foul of securities regulations.

If those evils do not outweigh the potential harm of leaving an employee in the dark, where do you draw the line? Would it be O.K. to tell an employee who is low on cash about a pending merger, so she could buy stock at the right time and get out of debt? Insider trading laws make the answer a clear no. But when the issue is ethical, rather than legal, judgment calls can be difficult.

The urge to stop a colleague from stepping off a financial cliff is natural, said Rushworth M. Kidder, founder of the Institute for Global Ethics in Camden, Maine, 'Here is a real live, breathing person whose whole life is tied up in this thing.' But, he added, 'you can't sacrifice the good of a great number of other people simply because you want to tell someone a little bit ahead of time.'

Heather J. Stone, president of the Murdock Group, a career training company in Salt Lake City, Utah, faced such a decision earlier this year when she had to lay off half of her 52 employees, including two who were house-hunting. She told one of them in advance, but the other 'did not have much career maturity,' Ms. Stone said, and 'would have a hard time' controlling the impulse to talk to other people.

'So I opted not to tell this person,' Ms. Stone added – even though she knew the employee had just made an offer on a house. 'No matter how much I want to share with the employee,' she reasoned, 'if the risk to the company is too high, I'm not going to do it.' Because Heather Stone owns her company, she has more latitude than most managers in making decisions.

Another solution may be to tiptoe between the conflicting principles of compassion and confidentiality, helping the employee make the better choice even when full disclosure is impossible. When my wife's former employer was planning layoffs, for example, she and many of her colleagues began searching for new jobs. When she landed one and went to give notice, her manager stopped her, saying, 'If you've gotten a new job, don't tell me.' My wife took the hint. She was laid off a week later and received a severance package that wouldn't have been available had she resigned.

'You have to come to terms with how to approach issues like this where you can't divulge all of the information, but to do it without lying,' Mr. Kidder said. He recalled a woman who once told him, 'I really find that I don't ever have to lie; I have too big a vocabulary.'

Dropping hints may help abide by the letter of one's duty of confidentiality, but it's hardly fair to limit disclosure to employees whose personal situation you know. A better approach might be to immunize the whole company against unpleasant surprises by persuading top management to share information more widely. In fact, a growing number of companies practice a more open style of management, teaching employees how the company makes money by sharing financial statements with them. Employees at such companies 'can see there are troubles and know enough about the business to understand when costs need to be cut,' said John Case, author of *Open-Book Management* (Harper Business, 1995).

If everyone knew about looming layoffs, as they did at my wife's company, rather than asking for advice about buying a house, an employee could probably discern for himself whether the timing was right.

16

In Dismissals, Silence Has Its Perils

The New York Times, OCTOBER 18, 1998

You walk into the office, and as the day goes on you realize that the guy who sat in the cubicle next to you for years isn't there. It's not just that he hasn't come in to work. There is no trace of him. The family pictures, the plants, the cartoons he had pinned up are simply gone. Office gossip has it that he has been dismissed. But there is no official word: no memo, no department email.

Welcome to the modern workplace, where companies are so concerned about wrongful-termination suits that silence often replaces honest communication. Most managers with the power to dismiss have faced the problem: whether to let people know why a colleague has been let go or to lie low.

A consequence of the first option is obvious: the risk of being sued for what may be seen as defamation. A consequence of the second may be subtler, but no less serious: creating a climate of fear and being labeled as a boss who does not level with the staff.

Who can blame companies for choosing the silent route? In 1997 alone, more than 50,000 wrongful-termination suits were filed in state and Federal courts, according to Edgewater Holdings, an insurer in Chicago, Illinois.

'The upshot is you get a workplace where the law has made speech dangerous,' remarked Walter K. Olson, a senior fellow at the Manhattan Institute and author of *The Excuse Factory: How Employment Law is Paralyzing the American Workplace* (Free Press, 1997).

One casualty on this battlefield was Paul J. McCarthy, dismissed in January 1994 by a Rochester, New York, division of Unisource Worldwide, a big marketer of paper and packaging systems. McCarthy had sold the unit's packaging machinery for almost four years. Unisource bought the company midway through his tenure. After initially being given no explanation for his dismissal, he said, he was later told that he failed to meet 'performance related criteria'.

Mr. McCarthy contends that he was dismissed because he told supervisors about conduct by a fellow employee that had put a Unisource vendor at a significant safety risk by taking him to a bad neighborhood. The vendor confirms that account, but did not report the incident to Unisource and declined to be identified.

'We sold over $1 million worth of product through his company,' the vendor said. 'I didn't want to risk losing the business.' But he did tell Mr. McCarthy, who was a friend. 'He went ballistic on it,' the vendor said. 'Paul's a pretty righteous person.'

Paul McCarthy reported the incident to a regional vice president. The vice president told McCarthy's boss to dismiss him, according to Mr. McCarthy and others involved.

Mr. McCarthy, 39 at the time, was not part of a 'protected class', like members of a minority group or older workers, that can sue over a retaliatory dismissal, if that is what occurred. Given New York law's adherence to the notion of 'employment at will', Unisource did not need to give a reason for dismissing him.

Patrick Farris, senior counsel at Unisource Worldwide's headquarters in Berwyn, Pennsylvania, said, 'The company is very comfortable with the decision that it made with respect to his termination.'

If there is no legal issue, where is the ethical problem? It's simple. Fear of being sued has led to a situation in which people treat one another badly. They don't talk, or they talk but don't say anything. But this may backfire, said Mary Dollarhide, a management lawyer. Consider a situation, she said, in which a worker in a protected class has been 'a lousy performer', and there has been no employer discrimination. 'You don't counsel them because you're afraid you're going to get stuck with some bogus lawsuit having to do with their protected status,' she said. 'When things deteriorate to where you have to fire this person, you're going to end up with an empty personnel file without a lick of evidence that anything was ever wrong.'

Not a lot of winners in that picture.

PART III

BOSSES

Bosses often set the tone for behavior in the workplace. While it's common for employees to enjoy bantering about a boss's shortcomings around the water cooler, the truth is the better a boss is at managing employees fairly, the more likely it is that employees will respect the boss. But because the boss is more often than not the center of attention, their actions can have a rippling effect through the organization. In Part III, each of the five chapters (columns) considers some aspect of the boss's role.

Two of the chapters look at the impact that a boss's duplicitous behavior can have on the entire workforce. In Chapter 18, 'When the Boss is a Stealth Bomber', is the story of a boss who undermines the work of one of his staff by pitting another employee against her. Chapter 20, 'Bosses Beware When Bending the Truth', looks at the effect lying can have and the message it sends out when a boss's actions seem to condone such behaviour.

The remaining chapters explore, from very different angles, how an employee should react when a boss is in trouble. Chapter 21, 'Saving a Life but Crossing a Line', tells the story of an incredibly altruistic act by an employee who donates a kidney to an ailing boss. But this chapter also explores the impact such an action can have on the workforce if the relationship between that employee and her boss is not discussed openly both before and after the incident. Chapter 19, 'When the Boss Tumbles', involves me personally and questions how I should have behaved when the person I reported to at the time was charged with inappropriate behavior. Finally, in Chapter 17, 'A Boss Saved Them. Should They Save Him?', looks at the story of Aaron Feuerstein, the C.E.O. of Malden Mills, who kept his employees on the payroll when his plant burned down in 1995. Now that he's in financial trouble, how much (if anything) do those employees whose livelihood he saved owe him?

17

A Boss Saved Them.
Should They Save Him?

The New York Times, JANUARY 20, 2002

After my first grandson, Evan, was born in 1998, a friend gave him a sage-green blanket made of Polartec fleece. The blanket was made by Malden Mills, the textile company in Lawrence, Massachusetts, that nearly burned to the ground on December 11, 1995. I hadn't noticed the blanket's label until November 2001, just after Malden Mills filed for Chapter 11 bankruptcy protection.

As the fire was raging in 1995, Aaron M. Feuerstein, the chief executive, decided to keep paying all of his out-of-work employees while he rebuilt the company, which is privately held. For his actions, Mr. Feuerstein, 76, was heralded as a hero, someone whose commitment to his employees and community went beyond any ethical obligation.

But by late 2001, the company had run short of cash. Its annual sales stagnated at $180 million, and its earnings dropped to nearly nothing from $35 million in 2000. Already in debt for $140 million worth of loans, Mr. Feuerstein asked his creditors for an additional $20 million to keep the company operating. They agreed, but only if he first filed for bankruptcy protection so that the new loans would receive priority payment should the company not survive. 'I begged them on my knees not to go into this chapter,' he admitted. But he recognized that it was the only way he could get the funds.

51

Given Aaron Feuerstein's magnanimous behavior in the past, are any of his constituents – employees, customers or the company's hometown – ethically obligated to help him now?

So far, none of his customers – manufacturers like L. L. Bean, Patagonia and North Face that use Polartec in their high-end garments – have left him. His union workers have agreed to a salary freeze until 2003 and are giving up paid personal days in 2002. He estimated that those and other concessions would save Malden Mills around $2 million.

He has also received letters of support, some including small donations. 'It's one thing [to receive support] when you have a fire and you decide to rebuild,' he remarked, but when a company is in Chapter 11, 'who would ever anticipate that you would have thousands of letters of encouragement from strangers?'

Mr. Feuerstein said he never expected anything in return for keeping his employees on the payroll in 1995. 'You're supposed to do what's right because it's right, not because there's a payoff,' he added. 'And so I don't expect anything of people.'

The question is: should he?

As part of its 'Polartec Promise' campaign started in December, the company is asking consumers to buy products made with Polartec fleece. These generally cost more than ones featuring fleece made in countries where labor costs are lower.

'Any individual certainly can do that,' said Jon P. Gunnemann, a social ethics professor at Emory University, Atlanta. 'But there's no moral obligation to do it. At some point, if you decide to live in a market system, you can't function that way. The only thing that's going to fix his problem is a profitable business.'

Aaron Feuerstein knows that. He said he's optimistic that the company will make a $19 million profit on revenue of $200 million this year (2002), despite another setback in January – when the company voluntarily recalled 15,000 electric blankets that had been distributed by Lands' End after one shorted out.[1]

Barbara Ley Toffler, an adjunct professor at Columbia University's Graduate School of Business who specializes in ethics, said 'caring is something we like to see', but she wondered 'if making enormous demands on his constituencies is the only way somebody like Feuerstein can be successful.'

It's difficult not to want Malden Mills to succeed. As stories abound of corporate executives paying themselves fat bonuses before filing for bankruptcy while leaving the retirement funds of rank-and-file employees eviscerated, we are desperate for business heroes like Mr. Feuerstein.

But did his lenders have an ethical obligation to grant him the new loan? Or his union employees to agree to concessions? Do we have an obligation to buy from Mr. Feuerstein simply because of his past good deeds?

Absolutely not, just as he had no obligation to keep paying his employees six years ago. For him, it was the right thing to do. Without obligation, his constituencies can now decide what's right – whether that means buying a North Face jacket lined with Polartec or a less expensive knockoff.

I, for one, have my eye on another blanket made of Polartec fleece for my new grandson, Lucas.

---

[1] In early October 2002, creditors began expressing doubts that Mr. Feuerstein's revenue projections were realistic. Ross Kerber in *The Boston Globe* (October 3, 2002) reported: 'He had Malden Mills' plan project sales growing from $183 million in 2003 to $250 million in 2012, chiefly based on its signature Polartec fleece fabric for outdoor jackets. ... GE [Capital Corp., one of Malden Mills' creditors] has concluded such figures are overly optimistic.' At the time of writing, Mr Feuerstein's and Malden Mills' future continues to be an uphill battle.

18

When the Boss is a Stealth Bomber

The New York Times, AUGUST 20, 2000

An anecdote in Kay Hammer's book, *Workplace Warrior: Insights and Advice for Winning on the Corporate Battlefield* (AMACOM, 2000) brought me up short. It seems that Kay once had a boss who set up a secret team of employees to develop a project that would replace work she had been doing. She didn't find out until the stealth project was presented as a *fait accompli* at a meeting of her entire division of 80 employees.

'It was awful,' Ms. Hammer said in an interview. 'One of the things I had to ask myself after that public humiliation was why somebody would have so much animosity toward me that they would do that.'

Kay Hammer's story struck me, because I had once been involved in a similar incident from the other side. I was the one asked by the boss to develop a project in secret that might supersede someone else's work.

What should an ethical person think when asked to operate behind a colleague's back?

On one level, it is perfectly reasonable for a boss to want to explore new ideas and find innovative solutions to business challenges, and to assign the work to whichever employee seems best suited to the task. And it often makes perfect sense to hold potentially disruptive experiments close to the chest until it is clear that they will bear fruit. So keeping some co-workers in the dark is not automatically unethical. It all depends on what the boss is up to.

'Surely, there are ways to negotiate an outcome that partakes of the boss's desire for confidentiality but engages the support of the employee,' remarked Rushworth M. Kidder, founder of the Institute for Global Ethics in Camden, Maine. 'But that will only happen if the motive behind the boss's action was up front and straightforward rather than deceptive or wily. Was the boss trying to get rid of the employee, but simply lacked the courage to say so?'

In highly politicized workplaces, discussions of such issues are often avoided on purpose. Instead, innuendo rules under the guise of 'an obvious necessity for secrecy' or 'for the sake of the good cause', said Laura L. Nash of the Center for the Study of Values in Public Life at Harvard University. 'When this is allowed, you create a business culture with upside-down values. There is a general sense that honesty about underhand tricks is more distasteful than the tricks themselves.'

By insisting on secrecy, Ms. Nash said, 'people begin to portray the deceived person as the enemy – the dysfunctional one who deserves to be blindsided.'

'This little mental trick,' she added, 'covers up their own participation in the deception.'

It's also a sop to cowardice.

Unethical bosses resort to this kind of tactic, warned Steven Berglas, a clinical psychologist who teaches at the Anderson School of Management at U.C.L.A., when they are afraid to confront subordinates about problems with their work. Instead, they scheme to achieve their ends indirectly, by pitting employees against one another.

Employees, naturally, tend to put what the boss wants ahead of the needs of fellow workers. That's what I did when my boss approached me, though I didn't realize it until I took the plan to another colleague for confidential feedback. My confidant's response was unambiguous: the whole thing smacked of unfairness.

Maybe he felt free to respond in that way because it was me asking, and not our boss. In any event, he immediately saw ethical implications that I hadn't acknowledged.

'Sunshine is a great disinfectant,' Laura Nash said. 'When such behavior is opened to scrutiny – even in a confidential setting – the stench becomes clear. If you can't develop a product internally without cannibalizing your own team members, there is something wrong with your managing or your morals – or both.'

Kay Hammer said in hindsight that had she been more attuned to the kind of person the boss was, she might have seen the ploy coming and left sooner. 'If you think the boss is a total jerk and he shouldn't be in this position, that's not productive,' she said. 'You're not going to fix him or thrive.'

Having learned the hard way, Ms. Hammer quit to start her own business, Evolutionary Technologies International of Austin, Texas, which sells software that helps dissimilar computers communicate.

I stopped peddling my own secret proposal as soon as my confidant expressed his discomfort, and the whole thing fizzled out. But now, after reading Ms. Hammer's story, I have to find the moral courage to call my old deceived colleague and apologize.

19

When the Boss Tumbles

The New York Times, JUNE 20, 1999

My boss is in trouble. Last November [1998], my third month as a fellow at the Harvard Divinity School, Ronald F. Thiemann, who brought me to the school, abruptly stepped down as dean to take an unexplained, and much whispered about, sabbatical.

The reason for his sudden departure emerged recently. It was reported that Mr. Thiemann had been asked to resign after pornographic images were found on the Harvard-owned computer he used in his Harvard-owned home when he asked Harvard technicians to add more memory.

In his 13 years as dean, Mr. Thiemann, an ordained Lutheran minister, had quadrupled the school's endowment and strengthened its faculty, hiring such luminaries as Cornel West. Yet after the reports in May 1999, he was pilloried in the national and campus press and was no longer seen on the Harvard campus. Mr. Thiemann, on leave, has made no comment on the episode.

My quandary will seem familiar to anyone who has had a boss tumble into some form of public embarrassment – the chief executive who is discovered to have been cheating on a spouse, say, or one who draws unwanted attention by being drunk in public. Do I stand by someone who has done his job well – in this case, defend Mr. Thiemann's right to view whatever he wants in the privacy of his own home? Or do I decry the man as someone who, because of his station, should be held to some higher standard?

The decision in such instances ought to be based on whether the person being knocked from his pedestal really did anything wrong. Particularly when it comes to sex, organizations often uphold higher standards than the rest of us – aware of our own foibles – care to impose. (How else to explain President Clinton's rising poll numbers during the impeachment proceedings?)

Reports about Mr. Thiemann indicated that none of the images on his computer involved children; there was no suggestion that any laws had been broken. So issues of right and wrong quickly became murky.

'There's widespread disagreement about the morality of pornography even among feminists,' said Janet Jakobsen, an assistant professor of religious studies at the University of Arizona, and, like me, a fellow at the Divinity School's Center for the Study of Values in Public Life. Indeed, in 1990, Harvard's Fogg Art Museum proudly exhibited Robert Mapplethorpe photographs, which some people consider pornographic, and a CD-ROM of Mapplethorpe's works is among the holdings at the Lamont Library in Harvard Yard, available for public viewing.

From the reports, it is hard to see a reason for Mr. Thiemann to have been forced out – except, perhaps, his having been caught simultaneously in the undertow of two cultural bogeymen: sex and the internet. Would Neil L. Rudenstine[1], Harvard's president, have asked for Mr. Thiemann's resignation if graphic magazines had been found in a desk that the dean sent out for refurbishing by university workers? What if illegal reproductions of copyrighted paintings had been found on his computer? Word of such an incident would have been unlikely even to make its way to Mr. Rudenstine. But word of sexual images on a computer, coupled with a man who bespeaks values in society and – bam – Mr. Thiemann is banned in Boston.

The real issue raised has less to do with computers or pornography than it does with scale and fairness. People should be punished for their actions and not for the positions they hold.

So what do I do now that my boss has crashed and burned in a very public way? It is a problem that any worker could face, because bosses, being people, are imperfect. I considered my choices: if I truly thought the dean's actions were immoral, then I should join in the pillorying. But if I believed the university's reaction was rooted in embarrassment that the dean got caught, I should say that as well.

And that is what I'm saying – namely, that the incident was remarkable only because it was embarrassing.

Mr. Thiemann's behavior had no impact, as far as I could tell, on his ability to do his job. It was only after the embarrassment of the reports that things went awry.

---

[1] Mr. Rudenstine retired as president of Harvard University in 2001.

Because someone embarrasses us this is no reason to condemn him. You have to wonder about the values of people who do.

20

Bosses Beware When Bending the Truth

The New York Times, DECEMBER 20, 1998

L ying has consequences – dire ones.

That became all too clear during the week of December 13, 1998, as President Clinton, accused of swearing to a lie, found his credibility shattered and his every move and motive suspect.

What applies to political leaders applies equally to business leaders. When Bill Gates appears to dance around the truth under oath in the Microsoft antitrust trial, his credibility, too, takes blows.

But actions of admired leaders like Mr. Gates and Mr. Clinton can do damage far beyond their own reputations. When a culture of lying with impunity is perceived to have taken hold at the top, it bodes ill for behavior in the rest of an organization.

'As long as there's this raging ambiguity and there's no accountability, people will start generating more and more lax responses to morally ambiguous situations,' warned Steven Berglas, a management consultant and a clinical psychologist at the Harvard Medical School. 'Most people will start lowering standards for what's tolerable. And that manifests itself in people going along with what's being reinforced. People are going to lie for expediency.'

Now, we are not talking here about a failure to tell every bit of the truth every waking minute, a feat that no mortal manages. Success in modern life is next to impossible without the maneuvering room afforded by a bit of calculated vagueness here and a strategically bitten tongue there.

'Not telling the full truth is different from outright lying,' said Joseph L. Badaracco Jr., professor of business ethics at the Harvard Business School and author of *Defining Moments: When Managers Must Choose Between Right and Right* (Harvard Business School Press, 1997). 'If you're going to run a big company or run the country, you can't put all your cards on the table; that's simply naive.

Life is a series of different games,' he continued, 'and you sort of play by the rules' when it comes to levels of candor in different circumstances.

Even fresh-faced business school students appear to distinguish between posturing and outright lying. In a recent [1998] survey at Ohio State and Harvard, M.B.A. students were asked to rate from 1 (bad) to 7 (good) the ethical appropriateness of various negotiating tactics. The students gave a rating of 5.84 to 'making an opening demand that is far greater than what one really hopes to settle for.' But they gave a much lower score, 1.99, to 'intentionally misrepresenting factual information to your opponent in order to support your negotiating arguments or position.'

There are also times when telling the whole truth is simply cruel, as when a doctor can choose whether to tell a dying patient in clinical detail how his health will decay. 'There's great room for discretion, for knowing when not to speak,' said Sissela Bok, author of *Lying: Moral Choice in Public and Private Life* (Vintage Books, 1989).

But discretion was not the better part of Mr. Gates's or Mr. Clinton's valor.

Spinning or denying uncomfortable facts and professing not to understand the definitions of simple English words – Mr. Gates wondered what 'concerned' meant, and Mr. Clinton famously construed 'is' – were more their pattern.

'From a managerial point of view, you should have a strong prejudice toward being clear, direct and honest,' because lying 'becomes a bad habit' commented Professor Badaracco. 'What is more, you might get caught. You set a bad example. The people who work with you probably aren't dumb; they'll copy what you do.'

Can either Mr. Clinton or Mr. Gates expect the whole truth from the people who work for them? A leadership policy of 'Do as I say, not as I do' cuts no ethical ice. And it probably wouldn't work anyway.

Once a leader blurs rules about what is acceptable – say, during sworn testimony on national TV – then no one knows the boundaries any more. Many in the rank and file will conclude that they are free to, and perhaps ought to, emulate the boss.

Alas, hubris often blinds powerful leaders and their followers to the seriousness of the damage. In the Clinton case, politicians fret most about the power calculus of impeachment and the Presidency; in the Microsoft case, executives worry most about competition, innovation and monopoly power.

But isn't there something much more important to fear – that each sworn lie by an admired leader will take the U.S. that one step closer to being a nation of liars?

21

Saving a Life but Crossing a Line

The New York Times, NOVEMBER 15, 1998

Art Helms, a software project manager for Applied Management Systems of Rockville, Maryland, must be one heck of a boss.

After Mr. Helms had spent three afternoons a week on dialysis for three and a half years, his doctors told him in May 1998 that his kidneys would have to be removed. He told his staff that after the operation, he would be on a waiting list for a donor kidney and expected to be out of the office for weeks. He never expected the reaction he received.

Nancy Nearing, a systems analyst at the company, offered him one of her kidneys.

'The gesture blew me away,' Art Helms said.

At first Mr. Helms didn't quite take her seriously. But Ms. Nearing did some research and determined that she was, indeed, a match. 'I don't think he was prepared for someone bouncing into his hospital room saying, "Guess what? We can do this,"' she said. 'And this was probably the first time I'd ever seen him outside of work.'

If they weren't close friends, why would Ms. Nearing, a mother of two who has worked 26 hours a week for the company since 1995, offer a kidney to her boss?

'You have a guy who does all the things you want a boss to do,' she explained. 'He gives you the tools you need to do your job right. He bends over backward to facilitate whatever schedule you need so that you can actually have a family life. Wouldn't you try to keep it going?'

One might ask where the ethical conundrum is in this extraordinary story. Clearly, Ms. Nearing's act is one of great altruism. Between July 14, 1998, when he had his kidneys removed, and September 10, 1998, when he received Ms. Nearing's, Art Helms experienced congestive heart failure twice. Essentially, Nancy Nearing saved her boss's life.

The ethical issue is implicit in Ms. Nearing's rationale for donating her kidney: she cares about Mr. Helms as a boss and wants to keep that relationship going. But her gift to Mr. Helms — which you would otherwise jump to call selfless — crossed many a workplace boundary.

And so her act of charity leaves tough questions in its wake: most bluntly, how does Mr. Helms ever fire Ms. Nearing, should the need arise? Less bluntly, how will the transplant affect work relationships?

Such matters can seem in poor taste, at best, and Mr. Helms and Ms. Nearing never discussed them. Neither did anyone else at the company. 'It never entered my mind,' said Margaret Hutchison, the director of administration, whom Ms. Nearing called to arrange for time off to recuperate.

The only time the issues came up was during a visit by Ms. Nearing to a psychiatrist, something that the Georgetown Medical Institute requires of donors before a transplant. Nancy Nearing was taken aback.

'They were really hung up on the fact that he was my manager,' she said of the hospital. 'It was uncomfortable, and it made me angry.'

The company should have discussed the issues with her and with Mr. Helms, advised Sharon Daloz Parks, a co-author of *Common Fire: Leading Lives of Commitment in a Complex World* (Beacon Press, 1997) and associate director of the Whidbey Institute, a career development group in Clinton, Washington. 'She is doing this in hopes that it preserves continuity in her work life, but if, in the future, she needs to be reviewed for any type of underperformance, who does that?' Ms. Parks asked. 'What happens if other workers begin to feel that she is in some way inadequate, but she's forever with us because she gave a kidney to the boss?'

Ms. Nearing does sense that something has changed in her relationship with Mr. Helms – that they and their families have grown closer. 'I'm not 100% sure Art would ever fire me if he had to,' she said. If she felt she was getting favors she didn't deserve, she added, 'then I'd have to go find another job – and I don't want to.'

Mr. Helms said he would be able to move Ms. Nearing to another job if, for example, she ever had a really tough year. 'That's my job,' he said. 'I hire and I fire.' But, he added, 'I had to make it clear to Nancy how much I appreciated what she did.'

Most people try to keep work and personal lives separate, even as the boundary grows murky. Many find it natural to discuss the implications of personal decisions with family members. Far fewer, it seems, have such talks with co-workers when they are the ones involved. But they should.

PART IV

PRIVACY

Increasingly, the issue of privacy and the use of technology has become the focal point of many heated discussions on what right individuals have to expect their behavior online to be considered private. The three chapters (columns) in Part IV take on this sensitive subject.

Chapters 22, 'As Office Snooping Grows, Who Watches the Watchers?', and 24, 'You've Got Mail. You're Being Watched', look at the issue of employee privacy, particularly in the area of email and Web use on the job. Chapter 22 considers the growing number of companies that say they monitor their employees while on the job and explores the impact of having someone whose job it is to monitor this activity. Chapter 24 uses a specific story, of a company where employees were fired for inappropriate use of technology, as a starting point to discuss how it remains a challenge for employers to convince employees that email is a totally different form of communication from casual conversation around the water cooler.

Chapter 23, 'Who is Minding Your Own Business?' reflects on the ethical considerations companies that track online behavior should take into account when deciding how much information they disclose to the people they're tracking.

22

As Office Snooping Grows,
Who Watches the Watchers?

The New York Times, JUNE 18, 2000

Except for the shouting, it is becoming clear that the debate over employee privacy is over.

The American Management Association conducts an annual survey on electronic monitoring and surveillance in the workplace, and the results, released in mid-2000, show that widespread, routine snooping on employees is no longer a threat but a fact. Nearly three-quarters of the large American companies that responded to the survey said they actively record and review at least one of the following: employees' phone calls, email, internet connections and computer files. That is twice as many as in 1997. And one company in four has fired an employee over what the surveillance uncovered.

So the ethical quandary over whether to monitor will soon be moot. Factors like fear of sexual harassment litigation, lost employee productivity and theft of proprietary data and software have swamped any hesitations about privacy. It is almost a dead certainty that your employer will be having a peek at what you're up to – if not today, then tomorrow.

If monitoring is a given, a new challenge for employers takes center stage: setting up a monitoring system that is ethical and fair to all employees, and not merely defensible in court.

A key issue, of course, is: who will do the monitoring? And that is where things get sticky.

Two approaches are possible. Monitoring could become a full-time job for a person or department, or it could be made a sideline among other responsibilities. Each approach presents problems.

When policing co-workers is someone's main job, human nature creates a real danger. The designated monitor will have every incentive to find problems to justify his or her job, said N. Ben Fairweather, a research fellow at the Centre for Computing and Social Responsibility in Leicester, England. Once the egregious offenders are weeded out, an effective monitoring program can easily devolve into a wild, self-perpetuating array of witch-hunts and speed traps – an ethically unjustifiable state of affairs, however one may feel about monitoring in the abstract.

More often, monitoring is assigned to people or departments that mainly do something else. Typically, the job goes to information technology people, for no better reason than that they are usually the only ones who have the necessary access to hardware and software and know how it all works, on the snoop's side as well as the user's.

But think again of human nature. Making snooping a sideline is likely to lead to wild inconsistencies, occasional incompetence or outright capriciousness in the way monitoring is applied and policies are enforced.

I don't mean to suggest that technical people are reckless or capricious. Only a fool would make such an observation and expect his office internet connection to work smoothly ever again.

It's just that the do-it-in-your-spare-time approach is doomed from the outset. People will naturally devote most of their time and attention to their principal responsibilities – the ones that figure in whether they get promotions and raises – and turn to monitoring only when they have the time and inclination. Inevitably, that means inconsistent enforcement, which can be worse than none at all.

'Generally, in all areas of corporate management, the idea of having a policy is a good one, but it's not enough,' noted Jeffrey D. Neuburger, a lawyer specializing in technology-related issues at Brown Raysman Millstein Felder & Steiner, a Manhattan firm. 'If you don't enforce it, you're almost better off not having a policy because you get charged with this standard that you're telling the world that you're going to live under.'

Mr. Neuberger's point is one both of fairness and of vulnerability in court. A company sued by an employee over a claim of sexual harassment can find itself in trouble, for example, if it can be demonstrated that the company adopted a policy against viewing internet pornography on office computers but did not consistently enforce the policy. It won't do much for the company's defense to have some harassed systems analyst testify that checking the logs for naughty downloads was item No. 137 on her weekly to-do list.

Another survey released in 2000 by Elron Software, a publisher of monitoring software, shows that internet policy enforcement is far from airtight. One-tenth of workers responding to the survey said they had seen co-workers viewing adult websites on the job; more than half of that 10% said their companies had explicit policies forbidding it.

If full-time snoops are prone to overzealousness and part-timers to inconsistency, what is the right way to manage routine monitoring? There isn't one.

The ethical approach is to use snooping the way the police are supposed to use searches and telephone taps: only when warranted. 'There might be a need for monitoring, but only after the organization has good grounds for suspecting that there is abuse,' Dr. Fairweather advised.

In other words, he snoops fairest who snoops least, and then only with cause.

23

Who is Minding Your Own Business?

The New York Times, MARCH 19, 2000

What does it mean to be ethical about privacy on the internet? Are good, or at least fairly harmless, intentions enough?

A firestorm of criticism descended in early 2000 on DoubleClick, the internet advertising and consumer data tracking firm, when it said it would begin linking its trove of hitherto anonymous data about people's internet activities with the real names, addresses and profiles of consumers in a database it had acquired. The outcry led the company to suspend its plans.

Kevin O'Connor, the chief executive of DoubleClick, said the problem was simply that 'we got ahead of ourselves' by moving before the industry had developed clear guidelines on privacy and data gathering.

Describing the information in the databases that were to be linked as 'very innocuous, like if I bought a sweater or something,' O'Connor said one of the reasons DoubleClick overreached was, in fact, that it is 'a very good company, a very ethical and moral company' that intended to help consumers by saving marketers money. 'The less people spend on marketing, the cheaper products are,' he said.

Critics saw it very differently. 'I'm appalled at DoubleClick's approach to this,' said David Shenk, a seasoned internet observer and the author of *Data Smog* (HarperCollins, 1997). 'It's clear they did it with no sensitivity whatsoever to people's privacy. They were just testing the waters to see if they could get away with it.'

But sincere or not, DoubleClick's we-mean-no-harm defense fails to get at the underlying ethical issues surrounding the assembling of dossiers on people for commercial gain.

DoubleClick and its competitors, which manage the banner ads that appear on websites – and while they are at it, take note of which sites you visited, which links you clicked on, what you bought and so on – do their tracking as invisibly as possible. Before the controversy over database linking, many internet users had no idea it went on.

And for all but the most technically adept, it remains next to impossible to tell when or by whom you are being tracked as you surf the Web. The vague privacy policy small print on most commercial websites is no help.

All this secrecy and obfuscation is a dead giveaway to a fundamental ethical problem: no informed consent. And that is by design, because when it comes to being spied on, the more people are informed, the less they consent.

DoubleClick allows people to 'opt out' of being tracked by using a page on its own site, but if you've never heard of DoubleClick, how would you know to visit it? DoubleClick's name appears nowhere on its clients' sites.

'When you go to somebody's Web page and you see a banner ad, there's no process there for the consumer to ever say anything,' said Lori Fena, chairwoman of TRUSTe, a non-profit organization that monitors websites.

Many people in the dotcom world don't see what the big deal is. 'The truth is that privacy protection is not really privacy protection; it's annoyance avoidance,' said Don Peppers, an author and marketing expert who also serves on DoubleClick's board. But when people are annoyed without any way of knowing who is invading their privacy, what data they are gathering, whether it is accurate, what will be done with it or how to stop it, it is only natural to see evil lurking.

Once the tracking goes beyond anonymous click trails and begins matching offline identities to online behavior, as DoubleClick and others may yet do, another ethical problem appears: how to keep 'tailored marketing' from drifting over the line into serious abuse.

'Forget whether you get served an annoying ad or not; it gets a lot more interesting when you start to deal with potential digital red-lining,' Fena said. The same database that permits a marketer to selectively send you ads for the same kind of sweater you bought last fall, can also be used to exclude you selectively from seeing attractive prices or offerings because, say, you've been seen to buy gangsta rap music online, or to visit Spanish-language sites, or have otherwise electronically flagged yourself as 'not our kind of customer'.

O'Connor would rather not use the word tracking for what his company does. 'I hate it,' he said. 'It's a pejorative term. We're not selling tracking services; we're selling advertising services.'

His wincing at 'tracking' highlights the conundrum facing businesses like his, not to mention their clients: how can they go on collecting powerful, potentially abusable information about people on the sly and still persuade themselves that they are respecting people's privacy – and doing them a favor besides?

'The ugly side of privacy loss is that which happens surreptitiously,' said Nicholas Negroponte, director of M.I.T.'s Media Lab. 'We trade privacy for various levels of personalization. What is annoying is when this happens without your knowing it.'

24

You've Got Mail.
You're Being Watched

The New York Times, JULY 18, 1999

'It was tragic,' recalled Mary Beth Heying, a principal at Edward Jones & Company, the brokerage firm in St. Louis, Missouri. In April 1999, an employee had complained to the human resources department after receiving an email containing inappropriate material, meaning off-color jokes, pornography and so on. 'We investigated and found that a large number of associates were involved' in distributing such messages, Ms. Heying said. Depending on 'the egregiousness of their involvement,' she said, the company dismissed 19, warned 41 and allowed 1 to resign.

The company has a 'very clear' written policy on email, Ms. Heying said. Some 2,700 of its 17,000 employees have email or internet access at work (none of the brokers do, because written communication is heavily regulated in the brokerage industry), and each of the 2,700 was given a copy of the policy when receiving email access, Ms. Heying said.

An American Management Association survey in 1999 found that 27% of companies do what Edward Jones does – monitor internal email – this is an increase from the 1998 level of 20.2%[1]. In the vast majority of cases, employees are informed of the surveillance.

---

[1] In its follow-up surveys of 2000 and 2001, the number of companies that monitored 'storage and review of email messages' jumped from 27% to 46%.

There is little doubt that companies have both the power and the legal right to monitor email sent on the company network on company time. But there are conflicting ethical imperatives at work when managers consider a monitoring policy: on the one hand, to avoid unwarranted intrusions into employees' privacy; on the other, to keep unchecked circulation of off-color jokes and other inappropriate material from creating a hostile atmosphere.

Allan A. Kennedy, a management consultant and co-author of *The New Corporate Cultures* (Perseus, 1999), starts from the premise that 'companies that monitor email traffic or use the power of modern technology to act as Big Brother to employees are dehumanizing the work environment.' Still, he sees a need for policing email, given how it can expose a company to litigation. He said the best approach is to let workers frame the policy.

'An employee-based email monitoring system would not be as disrespectful,' he pointed out. 'It would be from one employee to another, saying "We don't want to work in an environment where this kind of thing goes on." It'd be equivalent to the kind of natural monitoring that would have gone on around the water cooler.'

In reality, though, monitoring is rarely continuous; far more often it is used only when a company has someone or something to investigate – when, as at Edward Jones, an employee complains about a particular message. Indeed, Laura P. Hartman, a professor of business ethics at the University of Wisconsin, thinks the threat of monitoring may be seen as a sufficiently strong deterrent that companies can spare themselves from much actual monitoring.

Employers are naturally uneasy about unmasking inappropriate email and dismissing offenders.

But invasion of privacy isn't the root of the unease; the distress of firing is. Most managers dread having to do something so painful to the person across the desk. 'We have a zero tolerance policy with regard to inappropriate email, and people know that,' Ms. Heying said. 'Does that mean we didn't feel badly about 20 associates? Oh, by all means, we do.'

Email takes companies into new ethical territory, as they struggle with controlling a technology so utterly different from other communications tools. Unlike a phone call or hallway conversation, email leaves an audit trail that can pinpoint the abuser. But unlike a paper memo, email moves at lightning speed, both in delivery and in composition, often with little reflection or second thought. It will probably be a while before there is corporate consensus on the fairest balance between privacy and protection.

Until then, the responsibility to do the right thing falls upon employees, who can use common sense as a guide.

If an employee's passion for email privacy is born of a desire not to have the boss find out he's been placing bids all day for vintage comic books in an online auction, chances are he already knows he shouldn't be doing that at work.

In this new high-tech world, a remarkably old-fashioned rule of thumb applies: don't do what you wouldn't want to be caught doing.

PART V

LYING, CHEATING AND STEALING

Each of the chapters (columns) in Part V focuses on issues around some aspect of lying, cheating or stealing, and the impact these can have on a business.

Chapter 25, 'When the Truth Takes a Stretching Class', looks at the common practice that company owners employ when starting a business of stretching the truth a bit to make themselves seem more than they are, so that prospective customers will want to do business with them. Chapter 26, 'Lies Can Have a (Long) Life of Their Own', is about how small (or not so small) fabrications told about yourself can come back to haunt you. In Chapter 28, 'Telling the Truth, or at Least Most of It', I use a personal story to explore how much information you should reveal about yourself when you know that certain parts of it may reflect on you badly. And in Chapter 32, 'Storytelling Only Works if Tales Are True', the practice of storytelling as a management tool is discussed ... and how true the stories need to be to be effective.

Two chapters look at different aspects of cheating in business. In Chapter 30, 'Payroll Tax, Temptation and Trouble', the practice of trying to skimp on tax payments owed to the government, even when you're doing so to be able to keep a business running and keep employees paid, is discussed. Chapter 27, 'When Bribery is

Lost in Translation', explores how to navigate the issue of bribery when cultural differences find different forms of behavior acceptable.

Chapters 29, 'Big Theft, Small Theft: Is There a Difference?', and 31, 'Boundaries to Stealing All Those Bright Ideas', address the issue of stealing from two different angles. The first looks at whether you can or should draw sweeping conclusions about employees' behavior because of small infractions. And the second considers at what point a large company steps over the ethical line in gathering competitive information.

25

When the Truth Takes a Stretching Class

The New York Times, AUGUST 19, 2001

'It was a good article,' said Maria Bailey, the founder and chief executive of BlueSuitMom.com in Fort Lauderdale, Florida. 'The bad thing is I can't really show it to any of my clients.'

Ms. Bailey, 37, was talking about a short profile that appeared in the June 2001 issue of *Smart Money* magazine. In it, she recalled how she had made her company, a start-up website aimed at executive mothers, appear to be larger than it actually was. She told the reporter how she had added the names of freelancers and part-timers to the biographies in her business plan; used fake email addresses to give the impression that there were other people staffing her non-existent departments; and suggested to prospective clients that she had executives from companies like Blockbuster and Alamo on staff, when she had only received free consulting services from people there.

'I knew what I was capable of doing,' Ms. Bailey said in the article. 'I just had to sell them on what we were going to be.'

Ms. Bailey was forthcoming about the small lies she told to get her company going and concluded that a certain amount of such behavior 'is acceptable in business'.

She is certainly not alone in believing that truth-stretching is common in the start-up experience. 'It's central to the entrepreneurial process and unavoidable,' said Amar V. Bhidé, a professor at Columbia's Graduate School of Business and the author of *The Origin and Evolution of New Businesses* (Oxford University Press, 1999).

Even if you agree that such practices are commonplace among start-ups, a larger question looms: how far can the truth be stretched before an ethical line is crossed?

People who start companies often want to appear more established than they are. Unless you run a biotechnology company that has found a cure for cancer, Mr. Bhidé remarked, you have to do something to distinguish your business from all the other companies offering roughly the same thing. He suggested, however, that customers who fall for some truth-stretching tactics 'are also complicit in the process'.

'They want to do business with you,' he added. 'Part of them says: "Gee, I shouldn't do business with a start-up. If only that person would lie to me."'

Maria Bailey said she draws the line at certain things: committing to something that she cannot deliver, for example. 'Maybe it's because of my overconfidence,' she said, 'but I never put myself in the position of taking whatever I could get.'

But does having that kind of confidence in your abilities justify other kinds of behavior? From an ethical standpoint, of course not.

Confidence can cause an entrepreneur to rationalize lying to a leasing agent about his company's revenue to get premium space in a shopping mall. And it can justify pretending to be a doctor calling with a family emergency to get past a protective secretary.

Neither of these tactics was claimed by Ms. Bailey, but each was used by another start-up entrepreneur who described them to me as 'pretty innovative'. Most reasonable people would recognize his tactics as extreme and unethical.

Identifying appropriate and inappropriate behavior at the extremes is relatively simple, but it is the common behavior in the middle that becomes fuzzy.

Did Ms. Bailey overstep the line when she referred people to cathy@BlueSuitMom.com in human resources or debbie@BlueSuitMom.com in accounting when no such people worked there?

Problems arise only if you are caught stretching the truth. Would Ms. Bailey have come clean if a client had asked to speak with the fictitious Cathy or Debbie? 'To be quite honest with you, probably not,' she admitted.

That everyone is doing it is hardly a justification for lying. To behave differently may require business owners to dig deeper for a way to stand out from the crowd. But if lying has become *de rigueur*, what compelling reason is there not to join in?

Ms. Bailey said that she would not show the *Smart Money* article to clients even now, because it might make them suspicious. 'Are they going to read it and ask, "O.K., what part of what she's doing now is not real?"' she said.

That observation offers a compelling reason not to lie – namely, that once a deception is discovered, the egregiousness no longer matters if everything you do is suspect.

26

Lies Can Have a (Long) Life of Their Own

The New York Times, JUNE 16, 2002

Sandra Baldwin, the president of the United States Olympic Committee, resigned late in May 2002, a day after she acknowledged lying about her academic credentials.

Fabrication of information about one's academic past is hardly new. In its annual [2002] study of employee background verifications, Automatic Data Processing of Roseland, New Jersey, the provider of payroll and other human resources services, found that 41% of education records showed a difference between the information provided by an applicant and that reported by the educational institution.

Ms. Baldwin claimed to have graduated in 1962 from the University of Colorado with a degree in English, and in 1967 from Arizona State University with a doctorate in American literature. Only after Tori Peglar, who was preparing a profile of Sandra Baldwin for Colorado's alumni magazine, found discrepancies in fact-checking her background did Ms. Baldwin acknowledge that those facts were inaccurate. She had actually attended the University of Colorado for three years. She left in 1959 and completed her bachelor's degree at Arizona State in 1962. While she completed course work for her doctorate at Arizona State, she never wrote the required dissertation. Eventually, she taught English at Arizona State for 11 years, until leaving in the early 1980s to start a real estate firm in Phoenix.

Michael Moran, a spokesman for the United States Olympic Committee, said all of the committee's officers are volunteers. 'We've always relied on our volunteers to give us their biographical material,' he said. 'We didn't do a reference check on them.'

That policy, Mr. Moran said, will change as the group's executive committee seeks nominations for a new president. 'The nominees will be reviewed and checked by the ethics oversight commission,' he said.

The academic credentials on the resume apparently had no bearing on Ms. Baldwin's becoming president of the Olympic committee or on how she did the job. Neither are the credentials necessary for running her real estate firm. Why, then, should such lapses matter?

'You could say: "Come on, everybody lies,"' said Michael Josephson, president of the Josephson Institute of Ethics in Marina del Rey, California. 'Well, then, how come, when we are lied to, we are generally betrayed and outraged?'

Such lapses are significant because they call into question the character of any person who knowingly allows them to be perpetrated.

Ms. Baldwin declined to comment about her situation. But Lawrence Moore, a public relations professional in Phoenix who is acting as her spokesman, said, 'She does know that the materials on which those things were based were created almost two decades ago.' In other words, Ms. Baldwin had two decades to correct the mistake.

'Over a 20-year period, she certainly would have opportunities to modify her bio,' said Wendy Bliss, a human resources consultant in Colorado Springs, Colorado, who wrote *Legal, Effective References* (The Society for Human Resource Management, 2002). Bliss speculated that many people embellish their credentials because they think it is more impressive to create a history for themselves than to show how their actual accomplishments are positive.

Lying about academic credentials may pale next to the behavior of some chief executives and accountants in corporate America. People who lie about their academic past for a volunteer job are unlikely to find themselves charged with a crime.

But Sandra Baldwin's case is just the latest example of how small lies left uncorrected can take on a life of their own. More lies are told, or the truth is skirted, to protect the lies already told. The longer these go unchecked, the more a person's character is called into question when the truth is revealed.

'Corruptions start as a small ink stain that spreads,' Mr. Josephson said. 'We have to expect people of integrity to hold themselves to higher standards.'

True enough. Perhaps it's time for all of us to take a closer look at our resumes and biographies to make sure they're truthful – not out of fear of being caught, but because it's the right thing to do.

27

When Bribery is Lost in Translation

The New York Times, OCTOBER 15, 2000

Bribes are tricky. Well, not the bribes themselves. Deciding what constitutes a bribe and then whether you should pay one to do business in a foreign country – knowing full well that if you don't, a less ethical competitor might – can be the real quandary.

Washington hasn't made it any easier. Congress passed the Foreign Corrupt Practices Act in 1977, making it illegal for American companies to pay bribes to secure contracts in foreign countries. But the law leaves just enough ambiguity to allow for continued payments to oil the wheels. In permitting 'facilitating payments', the law recognizes that a small amount of cash might sometimes be needed to expedite what it calls 'routine governmental action'.

So, according to advice that the Justice and Commerce Departments offer on the internet, the American government is as likely as not to look the other way if a foreign government official is slipped a few dollars to process visas or work orders; provide police protection; ensure smooth mail, phone or power service; protect perishable product; or schedule inspections.

On the other hand, the government says 'routine governmental action does not include any decision by a foreign official to award new business or to continue business with a particular party.' (The full text of the government's advisory on the Foreign Corrupt Practices Act can be found at http://www.usdoj.gov/criminal/fraud/fcpa/dojdocb.htm.)

To some experts, that guidance seems perfectly clear. 'You don't need a law to know when you step over the mark between a facilitating payment and a real bribe,' said Frank Vogl, vice chairman of Transparency International, an organization that publishes an annual index that ranks countries from least to most corrupt, with the goal of increasing accountability.

But to others, the law merely disguises a bribe by calling it something else. 'What's silent here is that facilitating payments are still illegal in that country because they're bribes,' said Patrick J. Gnazzo, vice president for business practices at United Technologies in Hartford, Connecticut. 'And there isn't a country in the world that doesn't have a law on its books that says "you may not bribe my government officials".'

So if the law does not provide clear guidance, how can anyone decide how they ought to behave? In particular, what do you do if you're an executive from a country that is regularly ranked among the least corrupt (say, Finland) and you want to do business in a country that is regularly near the bottom of the list (say, Nigeria)?

The argument could be made that in notoriously corrupt countries, the best thing to do is to adopt the local cultural norms. After all, don't you owe it to your shareholders to do what needs doing and pay what needs paying to land a lucrative contract? And if you reject that idea, what victory is won for ethics if the host country simply decides instead to do business with your less ethical competitor?

'I've seen successful businesses who follow the policy "When in Rome do as the Romans do" 100%, and I've seen businesses who strictly adhere to their home country policies everywhere they operate,' said Walter Kuemmerle, an associate professor at Harvard Business School. 'Both of these types of businesses have been successful.'

But Professor Kuemmerle warned that 'it's generally better to stay out of corruption processes for good than to go into them just tentatively.'

'If the business decides to give in once' – assuming that it can rise above the morass later – 'that strategy is definitely not going to work,' he added. 'It's like a drug addiction. Once you signal that you're willing to play the game according to the local rules, it's very hard to reverse that policy.'

Mr. Gnazzo counsels taking a realistic view of doing business in a corrupt nation. 'Decide you're going to be patient,' he said. 'That means that your stuff may stay on the dock for a period of time. And you might not be able to get the product out as fast as you would like to.'

Even in countries perceived to be very corrupt, 'not everybody in that environment is corrupt,' Mr. Gnazzo added. 'That's a starting point.'

In the 1990s, United Technologies itself came under Justice Department investigation, though the department ultimately found no violation of the Foreign Corrupt Practices Act and dropped the matter. The action was spurred by a civil suit in which a former employee accused a United Technologies subsidiary of dismissing him for publicizing what he said were bribes to two Saudi princes to secure a contract; that case was settled out of court in 1993.

Then, as now, the company had a strict rule against making illegal payments to obtain business.

The author of an article in *The Economist* in 2000 described with satisfaction that while in the early 1990s it took bags of cash to get through customs in Nigeria, on his most recent trip he only needed to hand over a ballpoint pen.

But in the realm of corruption, such deflationary forces are rarely seen. In the bribery game the stakes are always rising. 'It goes up the next time and the next time and the next time,' Mr. Gnazzo warned.

Or, as Professor Kuemmerle put it, 'Corruption is a never-ending story.'

28

Telling the Truth, or at Least Most of It

The New York Times, MAY 21, 2000

When the results of an annual honesty and ethics poll were released last fall [1999] by the Gallup Organization, I had just begun a stint as a college professor and was feeling quite smug. There among the 10 professions ranked most honest by the American public was my new calling, with 52% of respondents judging its honesty as high or very high.

Then, after just a few minutes of basking in a professional glow, I saw that the survey ranked another of my incarnations, that of online journalist, firmly among the bottom 10 on the list of 45, with only one respondent in 10 giving people in that line of work a good score. Talk about professional disconnect.

The findings present a puzzle.

When introducing myself, what do I tell people I do? If I want them to trust me from the word go, do I just say 'college teacher' and withhold the part about writing for online publications?

If disclosing the complete picture leads people to draw an unfair conclusion about me, isn't it right, not to mention advantageous, to withhold some information? In a legal context, the answer is no. 'It's better to include and explain than to omit and cast doubt,' said Andrew J. Sherman, a lawyer at Katten Muchin Zavis in Washington, D.C. Of course, it is the job of a good lawyer to look through the lens of legal vulnerability and caution against anything that may lead to trouble.

But real life is rarely as straightforward.

Imagine that you are applying for a job during the McCarthyite 1950s. Years earlier, in college, you flirted briefly with radical politics. Should you disclose it and risk having the interviewer unfairly take you for a subversive, or hide it and be more sure of getting the fair treatment you deserve?

Those pernicious days are behind us, thankfully, but ethically analogous situations still crop up. A few years ago, when a colleague was on vacation in Northern Ireland, he wanted to rent a car and was asked the name of his employer (an American newspaper). The rental agent told him that the company could not rent to people in certain 'risky' occupations, including journalists.

My friend swallowed hard and pleaded, somewhat disingenuously, that his job – preparing maps, charts and diagrams for the newspaper – was really more that of a commercial artist than a journalist.

He got the car.

'We all practice selective disclosure,' said Daryl Koehn, director of the Center for Business Ethics at the University of St. Thomas in Houston, Texas. 'If we have been a professor at both Iowa State and the University of Chicago, we tell people we taught at the latter, because it is more prestigious. There is simply not enough time in the day to divulge our entire past history.'

The end has an impact on how we view the means. Sacrificing integrity to save a life is often, usually rightly, seen as heroic. Trimming the truth for personal gain – landing a plum contract, for instance – is difficult to justify. Somewhere in between is withholding true information that you think will lead people to false conclusions.

'We've stopped saying we are consultants, because as soon as we do, we find ourselves faced with a barrage of negativity and preconceived notions,' said Michelle L. Reina, co-author with her husband, Dennis, of *Trust and Betrayal in the Workplace* (Berrett-Koehler 1999). As well as being, well, consultants, the Reinas are principals of Chagnon & Reina Associates in Stowe, Vermont. Too often, Michelle said, people have difficulty separating individuals from professions and assume that any journalist is like all journalists, that any consultant is like all consultants. Now, she tells prospective clients that she 'works with organizations that want to bring trust into the workplace.' As words go, 'trust' strikes a better chord than 'consultant'.

Trust is also the key to solving the puzzle. Gallup polls notwithstanding, in all but the most extreme cases we simply cannot know with certainty how what we say will be perceived. Deciding to be less than honest about something trivial because we think the truth might provoke an unfair judgment of us is just a few steps away from deciding that deception for naked gain is appropriate any time we think we 'deserve' it.

'Trust by its very nature is an act of reasonable faith,' Professor Koehn said. 'It exists precisely because we cannot control all circumstances. We should not make the mistake of thinking that all trust is contingent upon full dis-closure.' When in doubt about how the facts will be perceived, she advised, look gently for more clues. Otherwise, she said, she would proceed on the assumption that most people can be trusted to draw fair conclusions about us, regardless of what we do for a living.

Good advice. Did I mention that I was an online journalist?

29

Big Theft, Small Theft: Is There a Difference?

The New York Times, NOVEMBER 21, 1999

Every Thanksgiving, as we prepare the dining room table, we get out our Spode china, the Reed & Barton silverware, the antique crystal and a small cloth bag that at last count held 36 mismatched silver butter knives I've swiped from fine hotels and restaurants.

I'm not particularly proud to admit that for the last 15 years or so, I've been 'collecting' butter knives as mementoes of fine meals or pleasant stays. I know my actions are wrong, and probably raise tariffs for the rest of you law-abiding citizens. But I also know that my actions are no indication that I'm likely to walk away from a hotel with one of its television sets.

Such a leap of theft hit me recently as I was working my way through one website after another, each devoted to employee theft. The numbers bandied about on these sites are staggering: businesses supposedly lose from $52 billion to $120 billion a year. But forget about trying to find solid proof for these numbers or even tracing them to an original source. And everything from vanishing pens to 'stolen time' to multimillion-dollar embezzlement is lumped together.

'Many of us are not completely legal,' said Laura P. Hartman, a professor of business ethics at the University of Wisconsin. 'There's no doubt that driving at 57 miles an hour in a 55-mile-an-hour zone is illegal. But violating that law doesn't make you the same as a child rapist. And when we categorize theft in the workplace as one big category, we are doing just that.'

Written policies at most companies draw no distinctions, barring employees from taking or using any company property, no matter how small, for personal purposes said Jay Hotchkiss, a Portland, Maine, consultant who helps companies write employee handbooks. But few try to enforce such policies down to the paper clip, he added.

Some business owners are resigned to petty theft by customers or employees. 'I own a restaurant and we've got these creamers for coffee that are cute little chickens,' said Scott Adams, whose main living comes from drawing the 'Dilbert' comic strip. 'The cream pours out of their little open beak. As soon as we got them they were a big hit and started disappearing like crazy. We were happy about it because anybody who steals a creamer obviously liked the restaurant.'

But Adams, whose first Dilbert book was *Build a Better Life by Stealing Office Supplies* (Andrew McMeel Publishing, 1994), said analyses of employee theft were always biased. 'They fail to take into account how much the employer has stolen from the employee,' he said. 'I don't know anybody who doesn't do as much work when they're not on the job. I've got a feeling the net of that is in favor of the employer.'

But basing ethical behavior on a tit-for-tat model can spiral out of control. Even consultants hired to stem the tide of theft say success depends on being reasonable, not puritanical. Rather than looking for petty 'borrowing' or Web surfing on company time, said Michael G. Kessler, a forensic accountant based in Manhattan, 'I'm looking for the person who's going to sit there and run his business out of my computer.'

Simply put, it is ludicrous to treat all infractions as if they had the same ethical outcome. Clearly, they do not. Not only is mutual respect lost if companies practice the petty rigidity of assigning every wrong the same punishment, but it can also have the perverse effect of provoking otherwise loyal, productive employees to up the stakes on what they will take from the office.

Reasonable solutions vary from company to company. American City Journals, a chain of city business newspapers based in Charlotte, North Carolina, states in its employee manual: 'Use of office equipment such as copy machines is allowed for incidental personal use and to further your commitment to non-profit and community activities.'

But while rules may make it easier for employees and employers to know what's allowed and what's not, no policy can anticipate every situation. It is better to create an ethical climate where employees see themselves as stewards trusted with some reasonable discretion over their use of the company's resources.

As for me, I've decided to end my days of knife-lifting. As I said, stealing is wrong. And who could possibly need more than three dozen butter knives?

30

Payroll Tax, Temptation
and Trouble

The New York Times, OCTOBER 17, 1999

It might be the most often-cut corner in starting up a business: putting off remitting payroll taxes to the Internal Revenue Service (I.R.S.). You don't have to talk to many veteran company founders to find one who has tried it – and probably regrets it.

'Entrepreneurs do a lot of things they have to do to keep going,' said Gregory Conigliaro, chief executive of Conigliaro Industries in Framingham, Massachusetts, which recycles paper, plastics, metal and glass. 'If they didn't, there would be a lot fewer companies around right now.'

Conigliaro, who started his company in 1990 when he was 26, fell behind on payroll taxes in 1992. Ultimately, after being notified by the I.R.S., he ended up owing $14,000, 'half of which was interest and penalties,' he noted. He paid that sum and has since been current on all his taxes.

There is considerable cash-flow pressure on owners of nascent businesses, and the quandaries can be painful: pay suppliers late and they cut you off, pay the landlord late and risk eviction, pay employees late and they walk out. It often comes down to who is the least likely to squawk – and the I.R.S., which generally doesn't know what you owe until you report it, is often the answer.

Months may go by before the tax authorities notice that they haven't heard from you, and by then you'll find the cash to make up the arrears – or at least it's easy to tell yourself so. It's a common self-deception.

On a practical level, taking a government 'loan' this way is risky. 'We try to counsel business owners that the government is the worst place you can imagine to "borrow" money from,' said Richard M. Colombik, a lawyer with International Tax Associates in Schaumburg, Illinois. 'You're paying a very high rate – interest plus a penalty. And they're the only creditor in the world that can seize your assets, garnish your bank account, and do it all without a court order.'

But there are bigger issues here. The choice not to forward to the government taxes withheld from employee paychecks, even if the alternatives appear worse, veers on to perilous ethical ground.

Some people distinguish between taking what was never theirs and being slow to relinquish what was once theirs but is no longer – and somehow rate the latter as not quite as bad. That thinking makes it easy to rationalize holding back the tax money for a while.

But it also shortens the leap to practices like diverting employee contributions to 401(k) retirement plans or failing to forward their health insurance premiums, actions whose dire consequences fall on the innocent.

Seeing a dangerous precedent, many business owners treat as anathema even the thought of using tax money as a source of emergency cash. 'For me, it's the same as walking into a store and stealing something,' said Christi Christich, who in 1985 founded Cristek Interconnects, a small company in Anaheim, California, that makes electronic connectors. 'And I'd feel much worse about stealing from my employees.'

Facing tough decisions, including ethical ones, is part of the territory for entrepreneurs, and it is only human nature for a business owner to seek the solution of least resistance. Temporarily diverting money withheld from employee paychecks can seem a seductively harmless short-term solution.

Though at best this taints the trust between employer and employee, and at worst spares the company one peril by exposing it to another, it can feel hard-hearted to condemn someone in a scramble to keep a company afloat for yielding to the temptation. Only when a revenue officer turns up demanding a reckoning does the wrongness of the decision come into focus.

Then, of course, the only solution is to pay up. 'You're holding these funds for the government, but you didn't give it to them, and the government does not take kindly to this,' Colombik warned, adding that the I.R.S. will aggressively pursue a business owner even if the company folds.

But the agency generally doesn't go after employees to make good, he said, and rarely resorts to prosecution. 'Most of the time, being a bad business person is not criminal,' Colombik said. 'If it was, we'd have a lot more people in jail.'

Like many business owners, Conigliaro has decided to have temptation removed from his hands. 'Probably the finest thing I ever did was switch over to a payroll service,' he said. 'Then you have no choice. The payroll tax comes out first.'

31

Boundaries to Stealing All Those Bright Ideas

The New York Times, JANUARY 17, 1999

To say that D. Clark Ogle is miffed is a wild understatement. His company, Johnston Industries, a $300 million textile manufacturer based in Columbus, Georgia, says that it has been the victim of corporate espionage. Outside consultants hired by a competitor, he contends, posed as a prospective investor and a graduate student to gain access to Johnston's trade secrets.

And not just any competitor, but Milliken & Company, a 16,000-employee giant that won a Malcolm Baldrige National Quality Award in 1989. 'Obviously, the things Milliken did hurt us,' said Mr. Ogle, Johnston's chief executive. 'They took away opportunities our people had found for niches we were exploiting somewhat on our own. Then, basically overnight, we had a competitor in there knowing our processes.'

Johnston is suing Milliken over the matter. Milliken has stated that it will defend itself 'vigorously' and that its long-standing policies forbid its employees or consultants from illegally obtaining proprietary information from competitors.

What irks Mr. Ogle most, though, is that Milliken takes pride in a corporate mantra often repeated by its chairman: 'steal shamelessly'.

According to Christopher E. Bogan, chief executive of Best Practices, a management consulting firm in Chapel Hill, North Carolina: 'The concept of "steal shamelessly" is really grounded on the concept of "don't be afraid to borrow". It's a dramatic statement that no individual, no company, no team, no industry can corner all good ideas. It doesn't for a minute suppose that you should steal proprietary information or trade secrets.'

Perhaps, but Mr. Ogle contends that couching the concept in words like 'steal' is just plain wrong. 'When you take something that has negative con-notations, just the subliminal message you send to your culture is different,' he said.

Tom Peters is not totally surprised by Johnston's allegations. Peters and Nancy K. Austin wrote about Milliken in A Passion for Excellence (Random House, 1985). 'From my experience, the ethical standard there is very high,' Mr. Peters said. 'But they are also a very aggressive company. If you have an action-at-all-costs mentality, even if your ethical standards are high, some-times people are pushed to do stuff they shouldn't have done.'

Is it possible to promote the kind of aggressiveness implied by the 'steal shamelessly' slogan without also promoting behavior that crosses the line into unethical or even illegal territory?

The original, benign meaning of 'steal shamelessly' may be lost on employ-ees new to the business world. In the 1980s, when the slogan took hold, most corporate cultures had a strong bias against anything 'not invented here', as the phrase went, and companies rarely acknowledged borrowing ideas from anyone, least of all rivals. Now, it is commonplace to grab others' good ideas, and even to share one's own.

'The good news is that people love to share stuff,' Mr. Peters said. The bad news is that if even one employee takes the phrase too literally, the rallying cry can seem like a dirty-tricks license.

Christopher Bogan, a co-author of Benchmarking for Best Practices (McGraw-Hill, 1994), a book about the practice of measuring and comparing a com-pany's methods and results against competitors', said, 'It's very easy to misinterpret what benchmarking is and what good it can provide for organizations, because people will wrongly think it condones illicit behavior.'

Preventing that misinterpretation is the challenge. It calls for making the keep-it-above-board message as loud and clear as the gung-ho, go-get-'em message.

Mr. Peters gave this advice: 'State your case very clearly: "Yes, we are aggressive. Yes, we are action-oriented. But if there's anything that ever shows up gray on your record, ethically speaking, you're either in serious trouble or you're out of here."'

For a manager, it is a useful test to ask yourself whether you'd have to fire someone if actions under consideration were ever found out. Milliken, in its statement, said it did just that, dismissing its consultants when 'claims were made about the propriety of the collection techniques being used.' But after-the-fact sanctions can be taken to mean 'Just don't get caught'. The message that some holds are barred needs to reach employees beforehand, with as much vigor as 'steal shamelessly' had in its nascence.

Perhaps the new slogan should be: 'Play hard, but play clean'.

32

Storytelling Only Works if
Tales Are True

The New York Times, NOVEMBER 19, 2000

'I was desperate,' said Stephen Denning, program director for knowledge
management of the World Bank. He had been trying to convince his colleagues of the importance of sharing knowledge throughout the organization.
But the persuasive tools he had used all of his professional life – analytical
charts and graphs, written reports – weren't working. So he decided to tell
them a story.

There was a health care worker in Kamana, Zambia, he said, who in 1995
was searching for a method to treat malaria. The worker logged on to the website of the Centers for Disease Control and within minutes found his answer.

The importance of having information collected in one place and available
to any World Bank worker in any out-of-the-way part of the world suddenly
became clear, said Mr. Denning, author of *The Springboard: How Storytelling
Ignites Action in Knowledge-Era Organizations* (Butterworth Heinemann, 2000).
By the following year, an organization-wide knowledge-sharing program was
put in place.

Storytelling can be an effective business tool. 'People just don't simply hear
stories,' said Joseph L. Badaracco Jr., a business ethics professor at Harvard
Business School. 'It triggers things – pictures, thoughts and associations – in
their minds.' That makes the stories 'more powerful and engaging,' he said.

The challenge for storytellers in business, however, is in knowing how far to go in embellishing the story to connect with an audience. Too often, the temptation may be to let exaggeration evolve into an out-and-out lie for the sake of the story.

'By telling a story, I don't mean "story" as in make things up,' said Robert Metcalfe, the retired founder of the 3Com Corporation. 'I have told the story of 3Com a thousand different ways. You make it dramatic. You select facts. You add drama. You wink. You smile. You leave out unimportant things that might weaken your point. It's all part of the gentle process of persuasion.

But,' Mr. Metcalfe added, 'one of my rules is: never lie.'

Crossing over the line to an outright lie can have devastating effects. 'I've seen people in organizations who really hung themselves with their troops by telling stories that were really quite different from everybody else's recollection,' said John Perry Barlow, co-founder of the Electronic Frontier Foundation and a former lyricist for the Grateful Dead.

It can be even more damaging if fabrications find their way outside the company and into the news. We've all seen how overstating a past achievement can wreak havoc on a political campaign – witness how much was made of Vice President Al Gore's storytelling during the [2000] presidential campaign. Such disclosures can throw a company into chaos while the truth sorts itself out.

'There are well-established rules about the difference between poetic license and downright prevarication,' Mr. Barlow said.

Of course, most who stretch the facts to the point of lying in the course of telling a story are unlikely to find themselves fodder for tomorrow's headlines. More likely the damage done will be among those within the company who can smell a false story.

Even those who are expert at using storytelling as a management tool have found that employees will pull them up on something when they have gone too far. David M. Armstrong, a member of the fourth generation to run Armstrong International – a maker of specialty steam products – and author of *Managing by Storying Around* (Doubleday, 1992), said that if you're telling a story about yourself 'there's less reason to be inaccurate, because you were there.'

Still, on one occasion, Mr. Armstrong recalled, an employee came up to him and said: 'David, you talk about working in the shop for two years. You spent two summers. It wasn't two years.'

'He was doing it more out of fun,' Mr. Armstrong said. Perhaps. But other employees who heard the story and had actually put in two full years on the shop floor might not have appreciated the elevation of summer work into a year-round effort.

The real challenge for any storyteller in business is to know that for the message of the story to ring true, the facts must have integrity as well.

PART VI

LEADING BY EXAMPLE

Each of the 14 chapters (columns) in Part VI explores some aspect of how individuals inside or outside corporations can lead by example and, in many cases, what the ensuing impact of their behaviors are on the business.

The story told in Chapter 33, 'A Blame Game Hurts Both Ford and Firestone', draws on the heated battle between Ford and Firestone over who was responsible for accidents involving the Ford Explorer and why each company's continued blaming of one another may have added to the damage already done by the accidents.

While a great deal of the popular writing on business ethics would have us believe that behaving ethically always translates into better business, clearly there are times when doing the right thing calls for actions that you know may harm the company's bottom line. Chapter 34, 'When Good Ethics Aren't Good Business', looks at this issue and uses the case of one C.E.O. who tried to do the right thing and paid for his actions.

Chapter 35, 'When to Go Along, and When to Walk Away', struggles with the topic of working for a company or organization whose principles go against your personal beliefs. In Chapter 36, 'Bad Behavior Can Be Perfectly Ethical', I use a personal story to try to address the growing tendency to label any behavior we don't like or don't agree with as unethical. Chapter 37, 'Survivor's Skills Work on an Island, but How About in the Office?' uses the television series 'Survivor' as a launching pad for a discussion about what type of behavior wins in the workplace.

The underlying story in Chapter 38, 'Throwing a Beanball in Business', is one of how much responsibility a company has to take when one of its star employees behaves inappropriately. The motivation for a company coming clean and admitting a mistake is at the center of Chapter 39, 'A Safer World for Corporate Mea Culpas'.

Chapter 40, 'How to Get a Company's Attention on Women's Pay', uses recent data that suggests executive women's pay not only continues to lag but has also dropped further behind that of men to discuss how to raise effectively this worrying disparity in the workplace. In Chapter 41, 'To Blow the Whistle, Drop the Mask', the decision about whether to disclose your identity or not when blowing the whistle on wrong behavior is weighed.

By looking at some of the behavior of businesses after the September 11, World Trade Center attack, Chapter 42, 'The "Me, Too" Mind-Set of Disaster Aid', explores the tendency of business owners occasionally to lose perspective when aid is being given. Chapter 43, 'Follow the Heart, or Toe the Line?', explores whether or when it might be appropriate to bend the rules if a more positive outcome is assured. Failure to take responsibility is common behavior when things go wrong. Chapter 44, 'In Bad Times, It's Easier to Blame', looks at how individuals might bear more responsibility than their words would suggest.

When management becomes aware that there is something that might cause harm to the company's employees, how real do the threats have to be before management share this with employees? Chapter 45, 'Managing Danger Responsibly: How Much Do You Tell?', looks at how some businesses have wrestled with this issue and how they've worked through the decision.

Finally, Chapter 46, 'Corporate Values Trickle Down From the Top', looks at how a C.E.O.'s actions speak louder than words, and how actions that don't mirror a pronouncement can undermine credibility.

33

A Blame Game Hurts Both Ford and Firestone

The New York Times, JUNE 17, 2001

Early on the morning of May 21, 2001, senior Ford Motor executives met with Bridgestone/Firestone officials at Firestone's headquarters in Nashville, Tennessee. Since the recall of 6.5 million Firestone tires on Ford Explorers in August 2000, after tire blowouts and vehicle rollovers, Ford had been analyzing the safety of the roughly 13 million Wilderness AT tires, made by Firestone, that were still in use on Explorers and Ford trucks. 'We wanted to get into a discussion at that time' about tire safety, said Ken Zino, a Ford spokesman.

Instead, John T. Lampe, the chief executive of Firestone, handed over a letter severing his company's 95-year-old link with Ford. The next day, Ford announced that it would replace those 13 million Firestone tires. 'We did not have confidence in the tire,' Mr. Zino said.

Firestone read Ford's motives differently. 'Ford steadfastly refused to look at the vehicle,' said Jill Bratina, a Firestone spokeswoman. 'We told them our concerns, asked them again to please look at the vehicle. They said no.'

Working out the purpose of all this public blaming isn't easy. In a survey of 130 of its members conducted in June 2001, the Council of Public Relations Firms found that 85% believed that Ford and Firestone could have avoided the damage to their credibility and consumer confidence if they had worked together rather than attacking each other publicly.

And from a legal standpoint – lawsuits are among each company's worries – the pointing of fingers at the supplier and then back at the manufacturer can be a mistake.

'It's counterintuitive,' remarked John D. Winter, a product liability lawyer with Patterson, Belknap, Webb & Tyler in Manhattan. When several defendants are involved in cases dealing with accusations of product liability, he added, 'it's usually a "united we stand, divided we fall" approach.'

After blaming a product's supplier, a manufacturer will have to convince a jury that it stopped using the product as soon as it became aware of problems.

From the public airing that Ford and Firestone have given their brawl, it would be too simple to conclude that blaming is always bad. Peter A. French, director of the Lincoln Center for Applied Ethics at Arizona State University and author of *The Virtues of Vengeance* (University Press of Kansas, 2001), calls it 'an act of moral courage'.

'The easier thing to do is to say, "Oh well, you know these things happen, too bad, live with it,"' he added. 'The more difficult thing is to say, "No these things happen because people did something inappropriate – something morally wrong, something wrong, period." And they need to be called to task for that. They need to take the responsibility and act appropriately.'

Indeed, in the Ford–Firestone fight, both companies have claimed moral motives for their actions. 'People will know that we took a moral and ethical stand,' Mr. Lampe said after the breakup. In response, Ford offered its own, more succinct, moral thrust. 'These are our customers and we will protect them,' Mr. Zino said.

But when each company vigorously fixes blame on the other, and when each claims the higher moral ground, it becomes nearly impossible to decide whose claims deserve more credence. Even in appearing to take some responsibility, each player casts more doubt on the other than it does on itself. 'We have taken responsibility for the tires that had the problems last year,' Ms.

Bratina said in June 2001. 'For the past 10 months they have been trying to divert attention from their vehicle on to our tires. We hoped that Ford would take responsibility for their part of this.'

At Ford, Ken Zino had his own take. 'Our customers are tired of us squabbling with a supplier,' he said. 'We sold them the vehicle. We will replace these tires.'

The real ethical lesson here is not that blaming is bad or good. Instead, the lesson is found in what happens when companies fail to work together to solve a problem after the marriage of their products. In the letter to Jacques Nasser[1], Ford's chief executive, in which he ended the relationship, Mr. Lampe wrote, 'Business relationships, like personal ones, are built upon trust and mutual respect.'

Jill Bratina elaborated, 'At this point in time, that trust has been damaged to a point where we can't continue working together.' When responsibility for a problem is not shared by companies, trust is lost not only between them, but also with their customers. After all, why should customers trust the statements of either company on safety issues when each has made it abundantly clear that it cannot even trust the other?

---

[1] Mr. Nasser resigned as C.E.O. of Ford in October 2001.

34

When Good Ethics Aren't Good Business

The New York Times, MARCH 18, 2001

Stories about courageous chief executives who, when faced with business pressures to do otherwise, choose to do the right thing invariably end up reading like morality tales. The message? Good ethics leads to good business results.

The fire that devastated Malden Mills just before Christmas 1995 was just such a story. Rather than collect the insurance money, lay employees off and shut down the textile company, Aaron Feuerstein, the owner, promised to keep the employees on the payroll while he rebuilt. Mr. Feuerstein rescued the business, saved about 3,000 jobs and kept the town of Lawrence, Massachusetts, where the company is based, from economic disaster.

While stories like Mr. Feuerstein's are inspiring, they add to the myth that good ethics and good business always go hand in hand. That is simply not the case.

'One could argue that responsible management and doing the right thing are often characterized by the same things,' Jon P. Gunnemann, a professor of social ethics at Emory University, Atlanta, said. 'But you can't infer that every decision about the right thing to do is necessarily going to be good for the company. Sometimes, doing the right thing can have tragic consequences.'

A prime example may involve Ed Shultz, the former chief executive of

Smith & Wesson, the gun manufacturer based in Springfield, Massachusetts. In March 2000, in an attempt to defuse lawsuits the company was facing from at least 29 municipalities that held handgun manufacturers responsible for violent crimes, Mr. Shultz entered into an agreement with the federal government. He said that Smith & Wesson would include locks on its handguns, research and implement 'smart-gun' technology that would only allow the owner of a gun to operate it and improve the way retailers sold its products. Much of this, said Mr. Shultz, was already being done.

'It was a business decision,' said Ken Jorgensen, a company spokesman. Tomkins P.L.C., the British company that owns Smith & Wesson, wanted to sell the company, a goal that was impossible as long as the lawsuits were pending. The company knew the reaction to the agreement with the federal government might be harsh. 'There wasn't any question there was going to be a hit,' Mr. Shultz said. 'The question was how big the hit would be and for how long.'

As it turns out, the hit was huge. The company was vilified by its customers, retailers and perhaps most vocally by the industry lobbying group, the National Rifle Association.

Sales dropped dramatically, and by October 2000, the company announced that it was laying off 125 of the 725 employees at its Springfield plant. Mr. Shultz left the company in September 2000, to run another company that had been sold by Tomkins.

Why would a company very publicly decide to implement changes in its products that it knew would likely meet with disapproval among its core constituents? Up until this time, Mr. Shultz said, the company had done everything required by the government in the manufacture of guns – no more, no less. But the decision to do more, he said, 'came because I couldn't answer the question, "Was I doing everything I knew how to do to prevent accidents?"' When he asked himself, 'Would I put locks on our guns if it might save one child? The answer was yes.'

'I had to make those decisions based on the tradition of the company and my own beliefs of what's right,' said Mr. Shultz, who still describes himself as 'a rabid gun owner'. He said the formal agreement made sense because Smith & Wesson was already doing most of what the municipalities were asking for.

In the short term, Smith & Wesson is suffering consequences that from a business standpoint might be considered tragic. What adds to the tragedy is that no other manufacturers followed Smith & Wesson's lead and the deal ultimately unraveled.

'Shultz may have done something that was in the best long-term interests of the company – making it seem like a corporate citizen and just doing the right thing – but since the law doesn't require others to do it, in the short run it may have hurt the company,' said Joseph W. Singer, a law professor at Harvard and author of *The Edges of the Field* (Beacon Press, 2000).

The thorny dilemma for company managers then is what to do when deciding between doing the right thing and doing what is best for the business. Ultimately, the ethical choice is clear: do the right thing regardless of whether you are rewarded for it.

'If you take your morality seriously,' Mr. Gunnemann said, 'then what's most important to you is not the bottom line, it's whether you can sleep at night.'

35

When to Go Along, and
When to Walk Away

The New York Times, FEBRUARY 18, 2001

As the attorney general, John Ashcroft is working for an organization that has some laws he finds disagreeable. His job, in fact, makes him the chief enforcer of those laws. Yet in his confirmation hearings, he said, 'I understand that being attorney general means enforcing the laws as they are written, not enforcing my personal preferences.'

Noble sentiments, perhaps, but his stance raises a difficult question: what are our obligations if we disagree with our own organization's policies or objectives?

Certainly, few of us will have to deal with such a quandary in a very public Senate confirmation hearing. For Mr. Ashcroft, it may be a simple-enough task to place the value of the law above his personal values. In the workplace, we often do not have the opportunity to use the law as a reason to suppress our true values.

Say you work for the production company that has created the 'Temptation Island' television series, in which nubile young singles try to coax partners in couples to betray their commitment to each other? There is nothing illegal about the premise, but if the idea of Bacchanalia and hedonism conflicts with your values, are you obliged to work on the show simply because your company has the assignment?

'If you are attached to almost any group, you will find some things internal to the group that are distasteful,' said Robert P. Lawry, a law professor and director of the Center for Professional Ethics at Case Western Reserve University in Cleveland, Ohio. In such situations, does an ethical person cause a scene? Leave the group? Or suffer in silence?

Such questions assume that most people have well-developed personal systems of ethics. That may not be so. 'It's a myth that there are all these autonomous principled thinkers walking around organizations,' said Linda Klebe Treviño, a professor of organizational behavior at Pennsylvania State University. 'It's just not true.'

If employees have no clear sense of what is right and wrong, it is unlikely that they will find themselves outraged enough to give notice over a particular moral issue. And while some people may take issue with a company that makes tobacco products or is involved in providing abortions, the vast majority of companies rarely face such issues. 'Most companies and most executives really look for the middle of the road and try to stay away from controversy,' remarked Joseph L. Badaracco Jr., a business ethics professor at Harvard Business School.

But what if you do have a highly evolved set of personal ethics? Even in situations in which your personal values are in conflict with those of your business, it is not a given that the right thing to do is to protest or flee. People's values tend not to change, but their priorities do. An 18-year-old in his first job may think nothing of quitting over a minor conflict, while an older worker may place more value on his family's financial security. So rather than run from conflict, some people stay in jobs and try either to shield themselves from the problem or to take a long-term view, doing what they can to bring about change.

At some point, an employee may decide that change is impossible. On a purely practical level, it is then best to leave. 'People aren't very effective as thorns,' Professor Badaracco advised. Unless one can accept the situation or hope to change it, there is no point in sticking around and becoming more agitated.

But staying in an organization that has values that clash with your own does not make you unethical. Even if you stay after claiming to have priorities that might have signaled your departure, no ethical breach is made.

What you do sacrifice if you stay under those circumstances is your integrity, warned Laura P. Hartman, a professor of business ethics at DePaul University in Chicago. 'And then people aren't going to trust you,' she added.

If your values clash with your organization's – whether you are on an island or in Washington, D.C. – and you have previously made it clear that, being the person of principle that you are, you would never stand for such policies or behavior, then you should leave. You should go not because it is unethical to stay, but because your integrity depends upon it.

36

Bad Behavior Can Be Perfectly Ethical

The New York Times, APRIL 16, 2000

I became furious recently with a company that held up paying a writing fee it owed me. I couldn't understand the delay.

I sent emails. I left phone messages. Eventually, an exasperated senior manager informed me that she'd been told there were 'problems' with the work I had done.

In fact, that was not the case. The manager had not spoken to the person with whom I had worked, only to an out-of-the-loop colleague, and had been misinformed.

Incensed, I told the whole ugly story to a friend. His reaction: 'That's just plain unethical of them.'

Well, not really. Sloppy, lazy or ignorant, perhaps; or more likely just a case of failing to ask the right person for the right piece of information. Ethics really didn't have anything to do with it.

My friend's comment, however, illustrates how often we use the word 'unethical' whenever someone does something we don't like.

Failing to return a phone call is rude. Storming off the job in a huff is impetuous. A demanding boss who expects far more from her charges than can possibly be accomplished in a working day is, perhaps, mean. But instead of calling those affronts by their proper names, we haul out the 'unethical' label – as if to make them more substantial, more severe, more deserving of condemnation. We want to dignify our discomfiture with a mantle of righteousness.

But painting every kind of bad behavior as a lapse in ethics cheapens a term that should be reserved for discussions of core moral values and their implications.

It's time to regroup. A good beginning would be to start carving out a thoughtful definition of 'ethical' by looking at what it is not.

Ethical does not always equal legal. It is possible to break a law – say, doing 40 in a 25 mph zone – and be perfectly ethical in the process, if for example speeding was necessary to get out of the way of an approaching ambulance. Conversely, unethical people have always found ways to do wrong even while adhering strictly to the law.

116

Ethical doesn't always equal nice, either. People can treat you rudely, veil their motives from you, shock you, inconvenience you or drive you nuts with their pig-headed intransigence without clocking up any automatic debits on the ethics register.

'We need to distinguish manners from ethics,' said Rushworth M. Kidder, president and founder of the Institute for Global Ethics in Camden, Maine. 'Some highly unmannerly people – Thoreau might have been so perceived – were deeply ethical. And some highly unethical people – one thinks of the Nazi commandant at Auschwitz – were models of good manners.'

Crying 'unethical' at every slight arises from a natural desire to win sympathy for a grievance. 'People are persuaded more by the word "ethics" than by "mean" or "nasty" or "rude,"' said Laura Hartman, a professor of ethics at the University of Wisconsin in Madison. 'We have come to a time in our society where we accept those latter qualities as part of doing business, while we have been told recently that unethical behavior should not be tolerated. It is far more persuasive to suggest that someone has been unethical than simply mean.'

It is also natural for people to paint their woes in the ways that are most likely to attract redress. Every mischance must be a treatable disease; there are no accidents, only negligence and malfeasance (on someone else's part, naturally). You can't get anyone to do much about someone who does something rude, but call the behavior unethical and, bingo, it's actionable.

This is not to say that meanness, rudeness, sloth, slovenliness, vulgarity or other obnoxious behavior *never* presents an ethical issue. Behavior so egregious that it tramples on the accepted values of a workplace might be considered unethical. But 'might' is the operative word.

Kidder sees in the conflation of ethics and manners both a cheapening and a backhanded compliment: evidence of greater attention being paid to ethics. 'If the currency of ethics has high value, it follows that those who want to denigrate something will be more apt to call it unethical than they once were,' he said.

Heightened awareness of ethics might be a good thing, but not at the cost of pulling the word's teeth. Better to save it for times when it is truly called for.

So, you see, when I relentlessly battered those people with messages and complaints until they finally coughed up my fee, I was not being unethical – just a pest.

37

Survivor's Skills Work on an Island, but How About in the Office?

nytimes.com, AUGUST 24, 2000

It's over. America's long love–hate affair with the first batch of castaways on CBS's 'Survivor' television series has come to an end. When the dust settled in August 2000, Richard Hatch, a corporate trainer from Newport, Rhode Island – who from day one wanted to get his tribe organized with a plan of action (so stated while perched in a tree while looking at the others set up camp) – was the winner of the $1 million grand prize.

But what happened on the concluding show has far-reaching implications for the world of work. Don't get me wrong. I'm not intending to graft a whole batch of socio-psychological-management-consultant doublespeak on to what was basically a well-fought and watched game. The contenders did that themselves.

In both the final two-hour episode and the one-hour reunion show (Reunion? Hey, we never knew you were gone!), the players chucked around words like work ethic, play ethically, values and morals with fevered pitch. Certainly, such stuff had been referenced throughout the series, particularly in Sue's diatribe at an earlier tribal council about how they weren't behaving any differently from politicians or corporate honchos who have to do what they do to get what they want.

The inference from all the banter is that the subterfuge, conniving, undermining and (add your own adjective here) behavior was a true reflection of what goes on in the business world day-in-day-out if you want to succeed. Hogwash!

Certainly, I'm not naïve enough to believe that such underhand behavior as Rich's consistent (and he was nothing if not consistent) devilish playing of one castaway against another to get what he wanted doesn't go on on a regular basis in the workplace (heck, I've worked with many folks of similar ilk and so have we all). But to suggest that such behavior is what makes the business world go round is absurd.

For one thing, if we're to believe some recent research, such uncivil behavior as exhibited by the ultimate Survivor hurts a company's bottom line. In 1998, Christine Pearson, a management professor at the University of North Carolina Chapel Hill's Kenan-Flagler Business School, conducted a study of 775 people who had been targets of incivility at work. (See the summary of her research findings at http://www.bullybusters.org/home/twd/bb/res/pearson.html).

Professor Pearson asked the respondents to fill out a 240-item questionnaire about the rudeness, insensitivity and disrespect that was inflicted on them by another worker. None of the incidents involved physical aggression or violence, but instead such things as undermining a colleague's credibility – an approach quite familiar to those on the idyllic island in the South China Sea.

Here's what the respondents told her they did after being on the receiving end of uncivil behavior:

28% lost work time avoiding the instigator.

53% lost work time worrying about the incident or future interactions.

37% believed that their commitment to the organization declined.

22% decreased their effort at work.

10% decreased the amount of time that they spent at work.

46% contemplated changing jobs to avoid the instigator.

12% actually changed jobs to avoid the instigator.

What's more, 94% of the victims said that they had described their encounters to someone else – most with workplace peers or family members, half with workplace superiors and friends outside of work, and about a fifth described the encounters to subordinates at work.

See if the characteristics of the uncivil instigators don't sound familiar: generally rude to peers, not respectful of subordinates, hard to get along with, emotionally responsive to problems, temperamental and 'sore losers'. Hard not to conjure up that image of Rich the nascent millionaire sulking after receiving votes at the tribal council to expunge his sorry manipulative butt back to the Ocean State.

And when you read Professor Pearson's finding that three out of four respondents believed that the instigator was good at 'kissing up' to superiors, who can forget Rich's attempt to get in the good graces of the CBS honchos on the one-hour reunion show?

So, apart from the fact that manipulative, uncivil behavior is certainly not conducive to a healthy workplace, what does all this say about Rich's claim that he played the game as ethically as he knew how?

Well, you have to give him marks for consistency. He drew up a set of ethics for himself at the outset and stuck to it like a fly to hog manure throughout. That's partly what worked against Kelly, the runner-up, who presented herself as being as wishy-washy in her final plea to the ousted castaway jury as she was throughout the show when she switched from one alliance to another and claimed to be morally conflicted by the time the show ran its course.

Morally conflicted? Hah! More like recognizing that her inconsistent behavior and attempts to get everyone to like her when they knew she'd just as likely be the one to turn the knife in them next was overtly transparent to her interlocutors. (There is a business lesson in Kelly's behavior. Managers who want everyone to like them and try to please everyone all the time instead of doing what's best for the company and all of its employees and other stakeholders are doomed to be viewed as wishy-washy nincompoops who garner little respect. Those who flip-flop constantly to protect their own flanks are equally reviled.)

Clearly, many of Rich's fellow not-quite survivors found virtue in his consistency. Does that mean he was ethical, or that a colleague at work who behaves in a manner consistent with his own set of ethics (and is clear about what those ethics are), is an ethical person? Does this suggest that simply because Rich feels comfortable reading about his antics in the headlines of the morning paper, it's a good bet his behavior was ethical? Hardly.

In his book, *Defining Moments* (Harvard Business School Press, 1997), Joseph L. Badaracco Jr., a professor of business ethics at Harvard Business school, makes the case that responsible 'people sometimes lie awake at night precisely because they have done the right thing. They understand that their decisions have real consequences, that success is not guaranteed, and that they will be held accountable for their decisions. They also understand that acting honorably and decently can, in some circumstances, complicate or damage a person's career. In short, if people like Hitler sometimes sleep well and people like Mother Teresa sometimes sleep badly, we can place little faith in simple sleep-test ethics.'

Oh for goodness sake, you might say, it's just a game. Chill out. These guys were simply doing everything they had to do to win the million smackers.

Absolutely true. It was a game and the tactics Rich used to play the game and win it all bear no more relevance to workplace behavior than would those of the winner of a Final Jeopardy question.

So don't believe the banter about work ethic, doing what's done in business every day and playing ethically. And don't for a minute think that Sue's final rant against Kelly reflects anything more than what Gervase so nicely articulated as being reflective of a 'sore loser'.

But I admit that I couldn't help but be suckered into the whole 'Survivor' thing (I missed the episode where Gretchen got booted; a heartbreaker if you ask me) from something of a business perspective. This has nothing to do with ethics or how business is run by a bunch of unscrupulous backstabbers.

It has more to do with, who among the final four I would most want to work with. The guy who played the game best and won it all in the end? Or 72-year-old monosyllabic former Navy Seal Rudy who, as his final words, answered the question about why he voted for Rich by saying, 'I gave him my word.'

I'm thinking that there's the guy whose ethics I'm more likely to trust. And, forget Richard Hatch, there's the guy we should want as a corporate trainer.

38

Throwing a Beanball in Business

The New York Times, JANUARY 16, 2000

The bigoted remarks that John Rocker of the Atlanta Braves baseball team made in a magazine interview have been widely reported. Mr. Rocker, a 25-year-old relief pitcher, lashed out at Asian drivers, the foreigners on Manhattan's streets, a subway-riding AIDS patient and a teammate whom he called a 'fat monkey'.

Perhaps without the added burden of tabloid headlines, many businesses face similar situations: a star employee's privately tolerated 'idiosyncrasies' spin out of control, and management must respond publicly. 'In the business world, there's a very good chance that somebody like this would be fired immediately,' said Joseph L. Badaracco Jr., professor of business ethics at the Harvard Business School. 'The hideous content of his views would badly damage the company's reputation, so they'd want to disassociate themselves.'

The team did not do that, though it had the right to, according to Jim Schultz, a spokesman for the Braves. 'John's remarks do merit some kind of discipline,' Mr. Schultz said. And Rocker showed some contrition in a televised interview last week. In any case, the matter is now out of the team's hands: Bud Selig, the baseball commissioner, has ordered Mr. Rocker to undergo psychological evaluation.

These are practical responses, damage control if you will. But what about

123

the ethics of the matter? Do the Braves have any business punishing a player whose on-field antics and volatile behavior have been tolerated by teammates and management until now, merely for escalating his rhetoric?

The team's conduct – summed up by the cynical observation, 'Do you know how hard it is to find good relief?' – certainly doesn't give management the moral high ground. But rationalizing idiosyncrasies in a star performer is common in business.

'There's a huge amount of hypocrisy insofar as there are no sanctions brought to bear on these people until such time as they gore the wrong ox,' remarked Dr. Steven Berglas, a clinical psychologist who teaches at the Anderson School of Management at U.C.L.A. If the Braves knew in advance about John Rocker's sentiments, he said, then they, too, must share some of the blame: 'Every time you look away, you're an enabler.'

When an employer accepts and sometimes even applauds star employees' behavior that most would find repugnant, it can lead to 'moral incoherence', noted Rushworth M. Kidder, founder of the Institute for Global Ethics in Camden, Maine. What is needed, he said, is the ability 'to think carefully from our moral premises to our moral conclusions and have a consistency about that.'

The inconsistency in the Rocker matter is clear: where was Major League Baseball's concern about his psychological state before his latest remarks hit the headlines? Much can be gained 'by having a courageous company step forward earlier rather than later and say, "We don't tolerate this kind of stuff,"' Mr. Kidder said. 'If we haven't established the fact that these things do matter, then again and again you'll find companies knowing what to do but waiting until the very last moment, because they don't quite dare act up front.'

Of course, there is an ethical case for a hands-off policy on the Braves' part: the man is entitled to his opinions, however odious, and to say them out loud in a free country; he is paid only to pitch. But tolerating the star's behavior means forfeiting any right to be shocked about it later.

Making Rocker undergo psychological testing seems more an act of political expediency than of ethical courage. And it may have unintended consequences: if the tests merely confirm that John Rocker is no different from thousands of Americans who share his biases, they accomplish nothing; if they detect a psychological problem, the team may be required to make some 'reasonable accommodation' for Mr. Rocker under the Americans With Disabilities Act.

Ethical consistency demanded a simpler and ultimately more honest response: 'Hey, the guy's comments are abhorrent, but get a load of his sinker.' Now, the best that can be hoped for is that the embarrassment of the incident will lead baseball to re-examine its tolerance of workplace bigotry.

Corporate cultures exist, Mr. Kidder observed, where 'it would simply have been telegraphed from the very beginning that you don't do that stuff here.' Sadly, the Braves and Major League Baseball have no such culture. Sadder still, many other workplaces will go on turning a blind eye towards unethical behavior by star employees, rising up in indignation only when public pressure demands it.

39

A Safer World for
Corporate Mea Culpas

The New York Times, MARCH 21, 1999

It was quite a headline: 'We Apologize!'

On February 25, 1999, the Colonial Pipeline Company of Atlanta, Georgia, used that large-type exclamation at the top of full-page advertisements in three newspapers, taking responsibility for an oil spill in 1996 on the Reedy River of South Carolina.

The advertisements, which together cost about $100,000, were part of a plea agreement the company reached with the Justice Department to settle criminal charges of violating the Clean Water Act. (The company also agreed to pay a $7 million fine.) The three short, contrite paragraphs of text in the ads were spelled out word for word in the plea deal, but the company chose on its own to add the headline.

The gesture took Ruth McQuade, the Government's lead counsel on the Colonial case, by surprise. 'When I went down and bought the paper, I said, "Holy Moses; this is quite impressive,"' she recalled.

But is the public too cynical to accept the sincerity of this act of corporate contrition? After all, the company, the nation's largest pipeline operator, had a lot to be contrite about: the Associated Press reported that the pipeline rupture killed 35,000 fish and polluted a 23-mile-long stretch of the river.

Noel Griese, a spokesman for Colonial, which is owned by ten large oil companies, said the company was merely trying to accept responsibility. 'We wanted to communicate the message that we had done wrong and that we're going to make an effort to see that this doesn't happen again,' he said. And from the outset, Ms. McQuade said, Colonial wanted to co-operate with the Government.

Before the 1990s, few companies would have dared to run such an ad, no matter how much they wanted to come clean. 'Historically, the U.S. legal system was somewhat hostile to apologies, because apologizing was equivalent to admitting error,' said Lynn S. Paine, a management professor at the Harvard Business School. 'You were opening this huge Pandora's box of potential liability.'

But in 1991, new Federal sentencing guidelines changed the equation. In cases where corporate defendants were accused of violating Federal laws, management's efforts to prevent misconduct or to take responsibility for it began to be taken into account when culpability was assessed. 'With these new guidelines, you have an incentive rather than a disincentive to apologize,' Professor Paine said.

At least in Colonial's case, the change seems to have had the desired effect. 'The exercise of a corporation trying to put moral emotion into what is essentially a legal statement is a good idea,' said Laura L. Nash, director of the Institute for Values-Centered Leadership at Harvard Divinity School. 'The word "apologize" even admits a sense of shame and humility, which is extraordinary for a corporation.'

It was extraordinary enough for the public to take notice. Pierre Ferrari, an Atlanta-based consultant and a director of Ben & Jerry's Homemade, the ice cream company, stapled his business card to a clipping of the ad, scrawled 'To CPC: Accepted' across the top and mailed it to Colonial.

'It's so rare for a company to admit their wrongdoing and then try to make amends,' Mr. Ferrari said. 'I thought the ad was very brave.'

Not all readers were as quick to accept the apology as genuine. 'The words are there, but I don't know that they're enough,' said Tochie Blad, an environmental activist in Atlanta who has followed the Colonial case and thinks that even more remedial action is needed. 'The apology only becomes valid if they follow it up' – by replacing the pipeline entirely.

Ms. Nash said she understands Blad's reservations.

'If the question is, "Should we instantly exonerate them?" I'd say no,' Ms. Nash said. 'They have to prove their new reputation. But there aren't a whole lot of mechanisms for corporate penitence, which is needed to begin to regain trust. And this was a signal that went straight for the jugular.'

Professor Paine said public policies that encourage apologies can also devalue them. 'The danger is that they just become pro forma, insincere and part of your public relations effort,' she said. 'For the apology to be effective, it has to go along with the corrective action and repair of the damages that have been done.'

Even then, will a jaded public buy it? It would be good to think that Colonial Pipeline is sincerely apologetic. It would also be good to think that people can accept a sincere apology without insisting on years of 'prove it' behavior first. A wall of cynicism hardly encourages companies that have strayed to take responsibility and make amends.[1]

---

[1] More than a year after Colonial Pipeline ran the full-page ads of apology, Bob Montgomery, an environmental writer with the *Greenville News* of South Carolina, reported on June 26, 2001: 'Five years after the Colonial Pipeline diesel fuel oil spill, those familiar with the conditions say the river's aquatic life has recovered and that the spill proved to be a blessing in some ways.' Vanita Washington, also with the *Greenville News*, reported on July 17, 2002, that 'Colonial paid the state $6.6 million for restoration of the river, and of that $3 million is set aside for the purchase of conservation easements.' Ms. Washington reported that conservation groups were negotiating to use the money paid by Colonial to purchase from owners 'a conservation easement to protect the area bordering the river.'

40

How to Get a Company's Attention on Women's Pay

The New York Times, MARCH 17, 2002

Women who are managers earn less money than their male counterparts. There's no shock there. But for decades, that salary gap has been shrinking – until now.

In a recently released study of the ten industries that employed the most women from 1995 to 2000, the General Accounting Office (G.A.O.) found that the gap between the salaries of men and women had widened for managers in seven of those sectors. The largest widening occurred in entertainment and recreational services, where female managers were earning just 62 cents for every dollar made by a male manager in 2000, down from 83 cents in 1995. Only three industries showed improvement for women – albeit slight. The biggest gain was in educational services, where the figure rose to 91 cents in the dollar, from 86 cents.

The G.A.O. report is supported by other studies, including one conducted by the Women's Research and Education Institute in Washington, D.C., showing that overall managerial salaries for women slipped to 71.3 cents in 2000 from 73 cents in 1995.

An obvious question arises from these findings: is it is ever ethically justifiable for executives, men or women, who make compensation decisions to pay women less than they pay men for doing exactly the same job? There's no gray area here. The answer is no.

Certainly, explanations can be found for the gap. 'Just because there is the presence of a wage gap, one should be hesitant to infer that there's discrimination going on,' said Elizabeth Owens, a government affairs manager for the Society for Human Resource Management in Alexandria, Virginia. 'A problem with these pay-gap studies is that they don't take into account individual choices that people make about what jobs they want and what they don't.' Some women, for example, may decide to work fewer hours to meet family needs.

Still, it's impossible to dismiss discrimination outright as a reason for the widening of the gap. Jared Bernstein, a senior economist at the Economic Policy Institute in Washington, D.C., said a study like this turns a spotlight on 'basic fairness issues'.

Variations in lifestyle choices might justify the existence of a wage gap. So, too, might the varying levels of experience and managerial responsibility that the G.A.O. study couldn't measure. What these factors don't explain, however, is why the gap has grown.

'The change is bad news for women,' said Heidi Hartmann, director of the Institute for Women's Policy Research in Washington, D.C. 'Women have been getting more education and staying in the labor market longer. Women are doing everything right, and still this is happening. Progress has stopped.'

Others say the slippage may result more from losing sight of the issue. 'I don't think it matters less to us,' said Laura P. Hartman, a business ethics professor at DePaul University in Chicago. 'But I think we've paid less attention to it and become complacent.'

Consider this, then, the sounding of an ethical alarm to stem the widening gap. But how?

For anyone who notices wage disparity in his or her company, the initial impulse may be to cause a scene by demanding equal pay for equal managerial jobs. But such loud noise may be counterproductive.

'This is a volatile issue,' warned Joseph L. Badaracco Jr., a business ethics professor at Harvard Business School and author of *Leading Quietly* (Harvard Business School Press, 2002). 'Most people don't like to be accused of being unfair, and they like it even less if you rub their face in it by documenting it. This is a minefield.'

The first step, he said, is to 'have some indication that there is a conspicuous disparity within your organization.'

'Without that,' he added, 'you're not going to get anywhere by waving a government study.'

Next, he suggested going to a couple of people within the organization whom you trust, to see if you have the facts right and to learn who else might be sympathetic to finding a solution.

The wage gap is the kind of issue 'where behind closed doors in a friendly rather than threatening way, and with analysis, somebody could make a case,' Professor Badaracco said. 'And the case is roughly, "Look, there are disparities; the women in the organization know about them. Things could get stirred up. We could get sued. Can we work together to find some way to move forward?"'

Ultimately, you have to go to someone who has the power to make changes. Regardless, Professor Badaracco said, 'you have to move with extreme caution.'

True enough. There's no upside to raising an issue in a way that creates only divisiveness. But doing something, cautiously or not, is imperative. It's unconscionable that women earn less as managers than they did five years ago. American business should be ashamed.

41

To Blow the Whistle, Drop the Mask

The New York Times, SEPTEMBER 19, 1999

Insiders who see something rotten occurring in a company or organization have a clear ethical obligation to speak up. But does that obligation include disclosing your identity?

It's easy to find reasons for wanting to remain anonymous. Consider what happened in the case of Jeffrey Wigand, who repaid Brown & Williamson Tobacco for firing him as head of research in 1993 by spilling some very embarrassing beans, including evidence that the company's chief executive, Thomas E. Sandefur Jr., who died in 1996, lied to Congress about what the company knew about tobacco's addictive properties. Wigand said a firestorm of invective and threats – both legal and physical – descended on him and his family.

By coming forward in a very public way, Wigand paved the way for the first successful litigation against the tobacco companies over the dangers of smoking. But he did so at a considerable personal price. Other potential whistle-blowers might look at his experience and say, 'I'll talk only if I can keep my name out of it'.

That may seem expedient, but it's the wrong way, for both practical and ethical reasons. In most cases, violent crimes being an obvious exception, the encouragement of anonymous whistle-blowing is misguided.

Start with the ethics: if you believe something is wrong and must change, anonymity should not be a prerequisite for coming forward. 'If the fear of retaliation causes us not to stand up for our principles,' said Stephen L. Carter, a Yale law professor and author of *Integrity* (Basic Books, 1996), 'then what kind of principles are they?'

They certainly won't be upheld by a complaint that gets ignored. And anonymous allegations are easily brushed aside as the work of someone with ignoble motives, like a disgruntled employee or a competitor.

Wigand's whistle-blowing had the effect it did because people could see that it came from someone in a position to know, said Terance D. Miethe, a professor of criminal justice at the University of Nevada at Las Vegas and the author of *Whistle-Blowing at Work* (Westview Press, 1999). 'The problem with anonymous reporting,' he said, 'is that usually no action is taken.'

Even advocacy groups set up to protect whistle-blowers, like the Government Accountability Project in Washington, D.C., recognize that the efficacy of complaints is tied to an identified source. Tom Devine, the project's legal director, said that he advises whistle-blowers to 'stay anonymous as long as possible' but that, sooner or later, 'if you truly want to make a difference, you're going to have to publicly bear witness and testify.'

Groups like Devine's exist because retaliation does occur. The Merit System Protection Board, a civil service panel, conducted a 1992 survey of nearly 1,500 federal employees who had reported what they saw as misconduct. Twenty-three percent said they had experienced verbal harassment or intimidation; one percent said they had been dismissed.

There is some legal protection for whistle-blowers under federal and state laws, but it generally applies only to those who report possible violations of laws to the authorities. If you report to top executives, say, that your boss is falsely claiming credit for another's work, you're on your own.

Even with statutory protection against official retaliation, there is nothing to stop co-workers from making a whistle-blower's life less than comfortable.

After all, no law can make people befriend those who take a righteous stand.

Moreover, some experts, including Miethe, believe that the laws themselves are a dismal failure. Unlike most lone employees, companies can afford to pay lawyers to hold up cases for years.

Patrick J. Gnazzo, vice president for business practices at United Technologies in Hartford, Connecticut, said he believes that companies can benefit from encouraging, not quashing, whistle-blowers. 'In a perfect world, an employee works for a company that wants to do the right thing, and the employee is not going to feel uncomfortable bringing things forward,' he said. 'The problem is, this isn't a perfect world.'

Though some companies try to create an atmosphere in which people feel comfortable and supported in identifying wrongdoing, the reality is that behaving ethically can wreak havoc on someone's life without any guarantee that wrongs will be righted. That is why those who speak up, despite the risks, are seen as courageous – and are believed. And it is why those who cloak themselves in what Carter calls 'a culture of anonymous complaining' often are not.

42

The 'Me, Too' Mind-Set of Disaster Aid

The New York Times, OCTOBER 21, 2001

'In a disaster, it's never fair,' said Pat Owens, the former mayor of Grand Forks, North Dakota, a city of 47,000 that was ravaged by floods in April 1997. 'You have to make the best choices you can with the dollars you have to work with.'

Ms. Owens, who was mayor from 1996 to 2000, was talking about decisions she had helped to make about which businesses would receive federal disaster money. Regardless of the criteria set forth, Ms. Owens said, ineligible businesses sought relief funds because they felt entitled to the same financial help received by others. 'There was nothing we could do,' Ms. Owens said. 'We just had to tell them they had to pull themselves up by their own bootstraps.'

In many ways, the devastation caused by the Grand Forks flood pales in comparison with that of the terrorist attacks on the World Trade Center and the Pentagon. But soon after the attacks – amid heroic rescue attempts, community support for displaced residents and workers, and myriad fund-raising efforts – cries of 'Me too!' began to be heard.

Tom Kershaw, founder of the Bull and Finch Pub in Boston, Massachusetts, the bar depicted in the television comedy 'Cheers', said he believes he is entitled to low-interest loans and other economic support because tourism, upon which his business relies, has softened. Mr. Kershaw claimed that before September 11, his business was 11% down on the same time the previous year. 'Now, it's about 50%,' he said. He attributes this directly to the attack.

'It doesn't matter in this case whether it's physical or not,' Mr. Kershaw said of the damage. 'The effect is the same. It's just a matter of intensity.'

As the airlines were 'jumping on Day 2' to cry for help, he said, 'the rest of us were just standing behind them.' In other words, if the airlines got theirs, Mr. Kershaw wanted his.

Perhaps a positive spin on that message, said Joseph L. Badaracco Jr., a business ethics professor at Harvard Business School, 'is that it's an issue of fairness rather than entitlement.'

But deeming that a pub 215 miles away from ground zero deserves similar treatment as the airlines whose planes were hijacked and used as missiles, just because its revenue is down, is a stretch. Even if a compelling case can be made, where do you draw the line? Many companies, while not affected physically, might say their customers stopped coming since September 11. 'As a practical matter,' Professor Badaracco said, 'I'm not sure we could sort out 20,000 companies and how badly they were affected and how much was caused by this problem or just bad management.'

Asked why he feels entitled to the same relief from public money as, say, someone whose business was physically destroyed in the World Trade Center attack, Mr. Kershaw said: 'It's my money. I can tell you about years when I gave the government a hell of a lot of money in taxes, and I'd like it back now, thank you very much.'

Mr. Kershaw, who is also chairman of the Greater Boston Convention and Visitors Bureau, contended that all business owners who could make an argument that their revenue declines were connected to September 11 should be eligible for some sort of relief. 'My big concern,' he said, 'is that there's probably not enough money to do this.'

Perhaps his commitment to protecting the financial health of his constituency of tourism-related businesses is obscuring the larger issue of deciding the right thing to do with limited resources. Such determination, however, rings hollow when others are more obviously in need.

'We had this horrible, unthinkable tragedy,' Professor Badaracco said. 'And here we have a guy with a successful bar that's going to have a couple of bad months. You know, what's he whining about?'

Mr. Kershaw also owns 75 Chestnut, a Boston restaurant that caters to a local clientele. 'It's holding its own,' he said. 'My local restaurant is not affected in a major way because people in fact are staying home.' He said he had already converted one of the rooms above the original Cheers into another bar catering to the local business as well. 'I'm proactively working on initiatives to build the business,' he said.

That's a smart management strategy. To people in New York who are still busy picking through the rubble of what were once their businesses, it must seem a luxury.

43

Follow the Heart, or Toe the Line?

The New York Times, SEPTEMBER 16, 2001

'We knew what was right,' said Samuel I. Schwartz, recalling the time in 1988 when, as deputy transportation commissioner of New York City, he decided to bypass budgeting-office procedures to repair the landmark Carroll Street Bridge in Brooklyn.

As a result of that decision, the bridge – the U.S.'s oldest wooden retractable span – reopened in time for its 100th anniversary, in 1989. If he had followed the rules, said Mr. Schwartz, who now heads the Sam Schwartz Company, an engineering firm in Manhattan, 'I would have had to wait until 1996 to open the bridge.' That was because he would have had to use money from a capital account instead of an expense account.

'We knew the community wanted this bridge,' he explained. The bridge was completed on time and under budget. For his efforts, the residents of the area heralded him. The budgeting office issued him a formal reprimand. 'I was used to it,' said Mr. Schwartz, now 53.

'I just apologized and moved on.'

The example raises a provocative question: when a system isn't working, is it ethical to break the rules to do the right thing – in effect, to get the job done?

The answer may seem simple enough. Who wants to admit to following orders blindly when asked why he or she complied with a rule that was part of a broken system? At worst, it conjures up visions of lives hanging in the balance while knowing parties remain silent.

For most of us, such issues are never as extreme. But they can catch us off guard when we follow rules we intuitively know to be wrong, simply because they have become generally accepted practice.

In the aftermath of the terrorist attack on September 11, it is likely that many people bent the usual rules to do the right thing and aid in the rescue effort.

Silent compliance can backfire. For example, one common rule within companies dictates that when giving references for former employees, supervisors should stick to the basics – confirming their employment and length of tenure (see Chapter 13 for more information).

In a 1997 case, the California Supreme Court ruled that an employer could be held liable for an omission in a reference. The case involved a school that neglected to mention to a prospective employer that its former vice principal had been accused of molesting a teenage student. The vice principal was subsequently accused of molesting a 13-year-old girl at his new school.[1] Common sense, of course, should have dictated that such information was relevant to pass along.

'We've lost the right for people to do what they believe,' said Philip K. Howard, a Manhattan lawyer and author of *The Lost Art of Drawing the Line* (Random House, 2001), an argument for people in authority to be able to use their own best judgment. 'The rules are debilitating. What we have instead is a culture that literally only works if people don't follow the rules.'

The trouble with rules, Mr. Howard said, is that in cases like that of Samuel Schwartz, 'they never honor the context of a particular situation.'

'They don't allow people to take into account their perceptions of what's really happening,' Mr. Howard added.

In 1999, an exhibit designer at a Boston museum encountered another way in which following the rules can get in the way of doing business. The designer, who was responsible for contracting out work to build exhibitions, found that the museum's accounting department routinely waited two or three months to pay its bills. That practice harmed many of the smaller contractors, he said, so instead of waiting, he would regularly pester the accounting department so that it would 'either feel bad for the little guy or just want to get rid of me' and pay the bill. 'A few times I submitted requests for payment long before I received an invoice,' he admitted.

Certainly, the best solution when rules get in the way of doing the right

---

[1] 'California Court Finds School Districts Negligent in Providing Recommendations,' *Human Resources Report* (BNA, Inc.), February 3, 1997. The case citation is Randi W. v. Muroc Joint Unified School District, Calif SuperCt, No. S051441, 1/27/97).

thing is to change them or, better yet, get rid of the corrupt systems that have developed around them. But most of us don't hold the power to overthrow systems that don't work. So people like Mr. Schwartz and the designer follow their own beliefs when the rules seem inappropriate.

If we all pick and choose the rules we want to follow, there is a risk of chaos. But we are not talking about willy-nilly rule-breaking here. 'Order is preferred to chaos except when order leads to unfair or unethical results,' said Laura P. Hartman, a professor of business ethics at DePaul University in Chicago.

Mr. Schwartz and his workers understood this. So did the designer, after being called repeatedly by a carpenter who was owed for work done months earlier. The designer finally bypassed accounting and called the museum president. 'One day later, I took a walk at lunchtime and hand-delivered a check,' he said. 'That was probably the most important thing I ever did there.'

There is, of course, no assurance that chaos won't result when rules are broken for a righteous act. But in such cases, as Professor Hartman said, 'perhaps chaos is the preferable existence.'

44

In Bad Times, It's Easier to Blame

The New York Times, MAY 19, 2002

In *The Grapes of Wrath*, John Steinbeck paints the scene of a farmer, carrying a shotgun, approaching the driver of a tractor that is demolishing his home. After the driver explains that a bank in Oklahoma City has instructed him to do the deed, the farmer exclaims in frustration, 'Who can we shoot?'

When things go wrong, our natural tendency is to find someone to blame.

Certainly, when corporations engage in fraud and deliberately deceive the public and the government, they deserve all the blame we care to heap upon them. But during the blame-heaping, we shouldn't let dissatisfaction with the way our own personal fortunes have devolved make us lose sight of who is really responsible for what.

If it turns out that Enron and Arthur Andersen were engaged in fraudulent accounting practices, then, ethically, we have a responsibility to hold them accountable. Similarly, if it turns out that stock analysts at Merrill Lynch let their business relationships affect how they rated stocks, then they should be held accountable as well. Indeed, Eliot L. Spitzer, the attorney general of New York, would have us believe that examples he lifted from thousands of subpoenaed email records from Merrill Lynch are the smoking gun proving that the company's internet analysts were deliberately touting stocks they thought were bad investments.

Timothy I. Cobb, Merrill Lynch's global head of media relations, said the email messages 'don't make us guilty.'

'It was just banter between colleagues, as you would around the water cooler,' he said.

Perhaps it's time for employees at brokerage houses to recognize that idle chatter suggesting contempt for investors and the companies they analyze might be overlooked when economic conditions are heady, but when the economy turns sour, such language becomes an easy target for blame.

'When stocks go up, there's very little complaining,' said James Wiggins, head of corporate communications for Merrill Lynch and Mr. Cobb's boss. But when the economy goes bad, the complaining starts. 'It's human nature,' Mr. Wiggins said.

Laura P. Hartman, a professor of business ethics at DePaul University in Chicago, Illinois, and editor of *Perspectives in Business Ethics* (McGraw-Hill, 2001), agrees. 'Our desire to praise is never as strong as our desire to blame,' she said. 'Blame is a natural, self-protecting tendency. Is it fair to blame Merrill Lynch, or do you take a responsibility in this? Given ourselves or someone else, we're far more likely to blame other people.'

David H. Komansky, chief executive of Merrill Lynch, told shareholders at their annual meeting in April 2002 that the company believes 'strongly in the integrity' of its research. He said the email messages 'that have come to light are very distressing and disappointing to us; they fall far short of our professional standards.' Some investors have been skeptical of his comments, because they were made only after Eliot Spitzer's office disclosed the contents of some subpoenaed messages.

Ethics come into play when considering the fairness of our judgments. 'All of us were happy to see our stock portfolios soar in value and did not want to look too closely at the practices that were generating our capital gains,' said Daryl Koehn, director of the Center for Business Ethics at the University of St. Thomas in Houston, Texas. 'When the market went south, we all looked for someone to scapegoat, instead of examining our own behavior. But I think more is going on here. Accountants will argue that more abuses occur during good times,' she said, because companies may not be as vigorous in following the processes they had established to ensure ethical behavior.

Similarly, when economic opportunities appear to abound, she warned, people are often willing to turn a blind eye to ethically questionable practices.

It is no surprise that when Americans are asked about their view of Wall Street, they are most approving when times are good. Thirteen percent said they had a great deal of confidence in Wall Street in 1995, while 18% said so in 1998, as the bull market continued. The figure jumped to 30% in 1999, in the headiest days of the dotcom rush, only to drop to 19% in 2002, according to annual surveys from the Harris Poll. Success, it seems, breeds confidence, ethics aside.

If placing blame is natural, then what is the lesson here? Perhaps it is that before we start firing away at the largest target in site, we should first examine how much personal responsibility we have in what went wrong and learn to hold businesses accountable in both strong and lean economic times. Then we should figure out ways to ensure that these fine messes don't happen again.

45

Managing Danger Responsibly: How Much Do You Tell?

The New York Times, DECEMBER 16, 2001

During times of uncertainty, company management has the responsibility, from a business and ethical standpoint, to manage that uncertainty.

The confusion can be debilitating, said Michael Useem, a management professor at the Wharton School of the University of Pennsylvania and the author of *Leading Up: How to Lead Your Boss So You Both Win* (Crown Business, 2001). 'It can be very costly,' he added. 'If people panic, they stop making good real-time active decisions.'

Since September 11, 2001, Professor Useem's comments have had a particular resonance. Frequent announcements from federal and state government officials of terrorism alerts have negated any notion of operating a business as usual. Managers have to wonder what additional responsibility they have to their employees.

The impact on a company's bottom line can be substantial. On November 1, 2001, after Governor Gray Davis of California suggested that state bridges might be targets of a terrorist attack, some companies allowed workers to stay at home the next day. Weeks passed and the bridges stood, but productivity across the region probably felt the wrath of terrorist threats that didn't occur.

'A generalized vague statement of that kind of a hazard would not create a legal responsibility on the part of an employer to keep his employees home,' said Baruch A. Fellner, an employment lawyer in the Washington, D.C., office of Gibson, Dunn & Crutcher. But legal responsibility aside, what is the best way to respond?

'We're mindful of the fact that the most secure employees are the best informed employees,' said David J. Manning, senior vice president for corporate affairs at KeySpan, a natural-gas company based in New York.

In other words, employees have the right to know about things that may potentially harm them so they can make their own decisions about how to act. 'There's a danger of puffed-up paternalism,' warned Thomas Donaldson, a business ethics professor at Wharton and the co-author, with Thomas W. Dunfee, of *Ties that Bind: A Social Contracts Approach to Business Ethics* (Harvard Business School Press, 1999). 'All too often, where a possible threat has been posed, managers conclude that since there's nothing that their employees can do to protect themselves anyway, there's no reason to say more about it because you might scare them unnecessarily.'

Employers, of course, have reason to try to avoid needlessly panicking employees. 'There does seem to be a point for most people where anxiety above a certain level just generates more anxiety,' said Dr. Arthur J. Barsky,

LEADING BY EXAMPLE

a psychiatry professor at Harvard Medical School who specializes in psycho-somatic illnesses.

While responses will vary from business to business, the most important action is for companies to control that which they can control. Companies should act reasonably, said Jay Neveloff, a real estate lawyer at Kramer Levin Naftalis & Frankel in New York, although he acknowledged that the concept could be 'horribly fuzzy'.

Security experts like Brian R. Hollstein of New Canaan, Connecticut, a security consultant who previously worked as head of security at Xerox and as an F.B.I. agent specializing in fighting terrorism, said no one in the secu-rity business wants to leave things to chance. 'But,' he said, 'the bottom line is that companies cannot do business from inside of a safe.'

If companies have a plan, their response to actual terrorism will appear rea-soned and logical. James P. Evans, chief executive of Best Western International, the hotel chain, said that while his company was not a victim of anthrax mailings, the company took the precaution of centralizing mail operations and having them handled by a small team of people wearing rub-ber gloves and masks.

'In my office, we've made sure to back up our computer system off site,' Mr. Neveloff said. 'We have collected home phone numbers, cell numbers, spouse cell numbers, email addresses and every conceivable way our employees can be contacted. We never thought to do that before.'

Many businesses had paid lip service to the importance of having disaster plans or backups of crucial information. Now the imperative of such pre-emp-tive actions has become clear.

Some ethicists believe that the events of September 11 and the subsequent threats will change the way Americans approach business and life in general. 'We will settle into a new frame of mind,' said Frank Navran, director of train-ing at the Ethics Resource Center, a non-profit ethics training organization in

145

Washington, D.C. The British and the Israelis have learned to be more alert in their daily lives to random terrorist acts, Mr. Navran said, and Americans will have to do the same.

'Life goes on,' he said. 'This is a period of adjustment and we will adjust.'

Perhaps that's true. But if businesses are looking for a positive aspect to these unfathomable events, it is that they will finally start doing all the things that ensure the safety of their employees and the continuity of their business that they should have been doing all along. The challenge is to continue on this path even if the acts and threats subside – while praying that they'll never need to use them.

46

Corporate Values Trickle Down From the Top

The New York Times, JULY 21, 2002

To: Mr. Steven A. Ballmer, chief executive of Microsoft

Re: Your email memo, 'Realizing Potential', sent to employees last month

I recently read your message to the 50,000 employees of Microsoft worldwide. What caught my eye was how much your message, at 2,674 words, noted the importance of values throughout the company and how you said that those values 'must shine through in all our interactions – in our work groups, across teams, with partners, within our industry and, most of all, with customers.'

You used all the right 'values' words: integrity, honesty, respect, trust, excellence and accountability, among others. But as far as I can tell, you cited only one substantive mechanism to show that all this talk about values is, as you put it, 'not just a fluffy statement of principles but really a guide to action': you said that 'starting with the upcoming August review, every employee will have a formal discussion of how they are doing on values with their managers.'

I applaud you for taking this step. But I'm afraid that you, like many other C.E.O.'s, haven't gone far enough. The notion that you want your company to stand for values is laudable, many ethics experts agree. But simply saying so and then asking employees how they are doing on the values front falls short.

'You've got to translate aspirations about values into specifics,' said Joseph L. Badaracco Jr., a business ethics professor at Harvard Business School and author of *Leading Quietly* (Harvard Business School Press, 2002). 'Otherwise managers aren't going to pay any attention to it.'

That's sage advice. Furthermore, how do you plan to balance the drive for innovation and big profits with the values of integrity, trust and so on? Clearly, there are times when these sets of values can conflict.

'He needs to put systems in place to ensure that the values-based culture is supported,' said Linda Klebe Treviño, a professor of organizational behavior at Pennsylvania State University. 'Probably most important is the reward system. How much does advancement and compensation depend on bottom-line performance versus the other values? And what happens to top performers who don't live by those values?'

But first, ask yourself to what standard you plan to hold *yourself*. Laura P. Hartman, a professor of business ethics at DePaul University in Chicago and editor of *Perspectives in Business Ethics* (McGraw-Hill, 2001), thinks that you are 'perhaps pointing the microscope in the wrong direction', given that most of the recent high-profile ethical problems in corporate America have been traced to the executive suite. Professor Hartman was not suggesting that Microsoft has suffered ethical lapses of late, but she contends that if you or any other C.E.O. want to instill certain values, you can start by acting as you'd like your workforce to act. That means making sure that your reports respond consistently to ethical quandaries and ensuring that incentives are in the right place. That would provide 'an actual commitment to these values rather than just an announcement about an actual commitment,' Professor Hartman said.

Then there is the whole antitrust mess, now crawling to a resolution in the courts. Less than two weeks after your memo was sent to employees, Judge Colleen Kollar-Kotelly of the Federal District Court in Washington, D.C., requested that you and the state attorneys general pursuing antitrust actions against Microsoft suggest areas of compromise when you made your closing arguments. Your lawyer's response was to suggest eliminating the concessions you'd already made to reach a settlement in the first place. That hardly smacks of the kinder, gentler Microsoft of your memo. A simple 'we can't come up with anything' would have sufficed.

Like many other chief executives, you have your work cut out for you to sell this values thing. Those who weren't already looking for reasons to criticize you will watch carefully to see if your actions belie your words. Here's my shorthand suggestion: take bold steps.

Set yourself apart from those high-profile corporations that are accused of financial wrongdoing. For starters, tell the world in plain English how

Microsoft constructs a clear, honest financial statement. Follow up by declaring that you already have some strong policies in place regarding possible conflicts of interest: having only outside directors serving on your board's compensation and audit committees, for example. Voluntarily adopt some of the corporate governance proposals now circulating, like the one that would rotate outside auditors every few years.

And if you really want to make a bold convincing stroke, follow the lead of Coca-Cola and announce that you're going to start treating all those stock options you hand out as expenses on your financial statement.

Try these things if you want the world to know about the compelling platform and clear mission as an industry leader that you envision in your memo.

You want people to know about Microsoft's values and what the company stands for? Show us.

Bibliography/Further Reading

The following works were cited throughout *The Right Thing: Conscience, Profit and Personal Responsibility in Today's Business*:

Adams, Scott. *Build a Better Life by Stealing Office Supplies*. Andrews McMeel Publishing, 1994.

Armstrong, David M. *Managing by Storying Around*. Doubleday, 1992.

Badaracco, Joseph L. Jr. *Defining Moments: When Managers Must Choose Between Right and Right*. Harvard Business School Press, 1997.

Badaracco, Joseph L. Jr. *Leading Quietly*. Harvard Business School Press, 2002.

Bhidé, Amar V. *The Origin and Evolution of New Businesses*. Oxford University Press, 1999.

Bliss, Wendy. *Legal, Effective References*. The Society for Human Resource Management, 2002.

Bogan, Christopher E., and English, Michael J. *Benchmarking for Best Practices*. McGraw-Hill, 1994.

Bok, Sissela. *Lying: Moral Choice in Public and Private Life*. Vintage Books, 1989.

Carter, Stephen L. *Integrity*. Basic Books, 1996.

Case, John. *Open-Book Management*. HarperBusiness, 1995.

Collins, James C., and Porras, Jerry I. *Built to Last*. HarperCollins, 1994.

Denning, Stephen. *The Springboard: How Storytelling Ignites Action in Knowledge-Era Organizations*. Butterworth Heinemann, 2000.

Donaldson, Thomas, and Dunfee, Thomas W. *Ties that Bind: A Social Contracts Approach to Business Ethics*. Harvard Business School Press, 1999.

Fraser, Jill Andresky. *White-Collar Sweatshop: The Deterioration of Work and Its Rewards in Corporate America*. Norton, 2001.

French, Peter A. *The Virtues of Vengeance*. University Press of Kansas, 2001.

Hammer, Kay. *Workplace Warrior: Insights and Advice for Winning on the Corporate Battlefield*. AMACOM, 2000.

Hartman, Laura P. *Perspectives in Business Ethics*, 2nd edition. McGraw-Hill, 2001.

Howard, Philip K. *The Lost Art of Drawing the Line*. Random House, 2001.

Kennedy, Allan A., and Deal, Terrence E. *The New Corporate Cultures*. Perseus, 1999.

Kidder, Rushworth. *How Good People Make Tough Choices: Resolving the Dilemmas of Ethical Living*, Fireside, 1996.

Miethe, Terance D. *Whistle-Blowing at Work*. Westview Press, 1999.

Mornell, Pierre. *45 Effective Ways for Hiring Smart!* Ten Speed Press, 1998.

Nash, Laura. *Good Intentions Aside*. Harvard Business School Press, 1990.

Olson, Walter K. *The Excuse Factory: How Employment Law is Paralyzing the American Workplace*. Free Press, 1997.

Parks, Sharon Daloz, Daloz, Laurent A., Keen, Cheryl H. and Keen, James P. *Common Fire: Leading Lives of Commitment in a Complex World*. Beacon Press, 1997.

Peters, Tom, and Austin, Nancy K. *A Passion for Excellence*. Random House, 1985.

Reina, Michelle L., and Reina, Dennis. *Trust and Betrayal in the Workplace*. Berrett-Koehler, 1999.

s7 READING

ion, Michael. *The Responsible Manager: Practical Strategies for Ethical Decision Making.* HarperCollins, 1990.

Shenk, David. *Data Smog.* HarperCollins, 1997.

Singer, Joseph W. *The Edges of the Field.* Beacon Press, 2000.

Treviño, Linda Klebe. *Managing Business Ethics*, 2nd edition. Wiley, 1999.

Useem, Michael. *Leading Up: How to Lead Your Boss So You Both Win.* Crown Business, 2001.

Other Sources of Information
on Business Ethics
(Websites, Associations, Resources)

The following resources were cited in *The Right Thing: Conscience, Profit and Personal Responsibility in Today's Business*:

The Centre for Computing and Social Responsibility (www.ccsr.cse.dmu.ac.uk), based at De Montfort University in Leicester, England, describes its mission as 'Addressing the social and ethical impacts of information and communication technologies through research, consultancy and education.'

The Corporate Library (www.thecorporatelibrary.com) is a research firm in Washington, D.C., that monitors corporate boards.

The Ethics Resource Center occasionally conducts a national business ethics survey. The results of its 2000 survey are online at: www.ethics.org/2000survey.html.

The Foreign Corrupt Practices Act is the U.S. law forbidding corporate bribery. The full text of the government's advisory on the Foreign Corrupt Practices Act can be found at www.usdoj.gov/criminal/fraud/fcpa/dojdocb.htm.

The [U.S.] Government Accountability Project focusing on whistle-blowing can be found online at www.whistleblower.org.

Harris Interactive (www.harrisinteractive.com), a research firm based in Rochester, New York, conducts the annual Harris Poll on corporate reputations.

Johnson & Johnson's Credo can be found online at: www.jnj.com/our_
company/our_credo/index.htm.

The Josephson Institute of Ethics (www.josephsoninstitute.org) is an
organization based in Marina del Rey, California, that does ethics
training.

The Society for Human Resource Management (www.shrm.org) is a trade
organization for human resources professionals based in Alexandria,
Virginia. Its website contains the results of many surveys the organization
has conducted of its membership.

Transparency International (www.transparency.org) publishes an annual
index that ranks countries based on their relative proclivity for
corruption.

TRUSTe (www.truste.com) describes itself as: 'An independent, non-profit
privacy initiative dedicated to building users' trust and confidence in the
internet and accelerating growth of the internet industry.'

Whidbey Institute (www.whidbeyinstitute.org) conducts leadership retreats
on Whidbey Island in Clinton, Washington.

Working Values (www.workingvalues.com) is an ethics training firm based
in Boston, Massachusetts.

The Workplace 'Incivility' Study conducted by Christine Pearson at the
University of North Carolina can be found online at:
www.bullybusters.org/home/twd/bb/res/pearson.html.